Where Angels Fear to Tread

Where Angels Fear to Tread

Confronting seven vital issues facing the church

O. S. Hawkins

BROADMAN PRESS
Nashville, Tennessee

4255-38
ISBN: 0-8054-5538-8

Unless otherwise indicated, Scripture quotations are from the King James
Version of the Bible. Quotations marked NASB are from the *New American
Standard Bible*. Copyright © The Lockman Foundation, 1960, 1962, 1963, 1968,
1971, 1972, 1973, 1975, 1977. Used by permission.

Dewey Decimal Classification: 261
Subject heading: CHRISTIANITY AND CURRENT ISSUES
Library of Congress Catalog Card Number: 83-24022
Printed in the United States of America

Library of Congress Cataloging in Publication Data

Hawkins, O. S.
  Where angels fear to tread.

  1. Christianity—20th century.   2. Theology.
I. Title.
BR121.2.H356 1984   230   83-24022
ISBN 0-8054-5538-8

Dedicated
To my Father in the Ministry, now in heaven,
DR. W. FRED SWANK

. . . He pastored the Sagamore Hill Baptist Church in Fort
Worth, Texas, for forty-three years.

. . . He led me to Jesus when I was seventeen years of age.

. . . He always had time for me.

. . . He taught me to love the Savior, love the saints, love the
sinners, and to love hard work.

. . . He showed me by example never to use my people to
build my ministry but always to use my ministry to build
my people.

In a very real sense—whatever I may be or do—is simply an
extension of what he was!

And, oh yes, those of us who knew him personally are aware
that he had a unique way of teaching all his "preacher boys" to
barge right on in . . . *Where Angels Fear to Tread*!

Contents

Introduction

Alexander Pope, English essayist of long ago, wrote: "For fools rush in where angels fear to tread." Songwriters later picked up on his observation. If not angels, it seems there are some critical areas where many Christians of our generation fear to tread. Too long the church has resounded with the 'sounds of silence' regarding several crucial, and often controversial, issues with which lay people are wrestling outside the four walls of our stained-glass "sanctuaries." Among these often-avoided issues are divorce, the poor, sickness, finances, and even the Bible itself.

People in the pews are looking elsewhere for answers to life's critical questions. They deserve to hear a sure and definitive word from our pulpits, a "thus saith the Lord." In a day when there are too many emaciated question marks in our churches, our people are crying for more authoritative exclamation points!

At the risk of being looked upon as a "fool who rushes in" and with the comfort and encouragement that the apostle Paul himself was a "fool for Christ's sake," let's begin the journey, *where angels fear to tread*!

O. S. HAWKINS
FORT LAUDERDALE, FLORIDA

1.
The Bible: God's Inspired Word

All scripture is given by inspiration of God, and is profitable for doctrine, for reproof, for correction, for instruction in righteousness: That the man of God may be perfect, throughly furnished unto all good works (2 Tim. 3:16-17).

Seldom do I open the Bible, the Word of God, to the people of God without recalling a life-transforming experience which occurred when I was a college student new in the faith.

Hurricane Beulah had swept through Mexico and left thousands of people homeless and destitute. I along with several other young men journeyed "south of the border" to see if we could help in rebuilding those broken hearts and homes. We spent our days handing out food and supplies to the homeless Mexicans along the levee area of Matamoros. We helped them rebuild their broken homes, often finding only cardboard for construction material.

In each village we would hand out Spanish New Testaments to humble people who were deeply appreciative of having a copy of God's Word for their very own. After ministering in the final village, we began to distribute New Testaments. Literally dozens of people surrounded us with empty-looking faces, arms outstretched, crying for a copy of the Word of God.

I shall never forget reaching into the box to pick out our last New Testament. After placing it into one of the many extended hands, I remember looking into the bronzed face of a middle-aged man wearing a worn-out straw hat. To this very day I can vividly see that look of desperation on his face. He longed to have a personal copy of God's Word which I had so many times before taken for granted.

To me, that Mexican man represents millions of people across the world who have never read a Bible, many of whom have never had it translated into their dialect. I have not been the same since seeing that man's face, and since that day I have tried to give thanks and show reverence for the Word of God each time I have opened it.

I wish you and I could travel together to Jerusalem, particularly to the Western Wall of Herod's Temple, commonly referred to as the "Wailing Wall." There we would see several old rabbis with long, flowing beards, their heads covered with skull caps or fur hats, and we would watch as they prayed and wept. Before they opened their Bibles to read the Psalms and pray, we would see them kiss each page before going to the next one. Upon the conclusion of their daily reading, as they closed the Word of God, they again kissed it, demonstrating great reverence for God's Holy Word. We are so prone to approach God's Word without the proper respect and appreciation afforded it. Jesus respected the Word of God. We read in Luke 4:16, "As his custom was, he went into the synagogue on the sabbath day, and stood up for to read."

As I come to examine "The Bible: God's Inspired Word," I do so with tremendous respect, appreciation, and love. The Scriptures speak of themselves.

All scripture is given by inspiration of God, and is profitable for doctrine, for reproof, for correction, for instruction in righteousness: That the man of God may be perfect, throughly furnished unto all good works (2 Tim. 3:16-17).

There is considerable discussion today, as there has been off and on throughout Christian history, concerning how the Bible was inspired. People are also debating and questioning over the issue of whether the Bible is without error or whether indeed the Bible contains errors. "The Baptist Faith and Message" statement adopted by the Southern Baptist Convention has accurately and uncompromisingly pro-

claimed that the Bible is "truth, without any mixture of error."
I believe that with all of my being.

It seems that today the Bible is not so much openly attacked
as it is subtly undermined. Is the discussion of the Bible's
authority a critical issue? Some claim that we should move on
from this discussion to focus all our attention on evangelism
and missions, but there can be no biblically based evangelism
or missions which are not founded and supported upon the
absolute trustworthiness of the Word of the living God. God,
through his Holy Spirit, not only breathed out the original
inerrant autographs but has preserved his truth through the
centuries.

If the Bible is not without error, then it must have at least
one error somewhere. Now if we could all agree on where
this particular error is found, the problem would diminish
significantly. If there are several errors, my question is: How
can we trust the Bible at all? My point is: the Bible is either
with error or without error.

Most so-called errors are easily explained away. Examine,
for example, the case of the healing of blind Bartimaeus of
Jericho. Matthew's account states that our Lord healed two
blind men in Jericho on his way to Jerusalem. The other
accounts of this event, Mark and Luke, mention that one man
was healed in Jericho. On the surface it appears that one of
the writers was at error. Now, the obvious truth is: if Mark or
Luke had said *only one* blind man was healed, there would be
a case for error. But in a crowd the size of one that normally
traveled with Jesus, perhaps Bartimaeus was well ahead of
the disciples. It wouldn't be unusual, therefore, for one of the
writers to report the healing of Bartimaeus only. But what
really happened? This could best be answered by an illustration. Suppose that you and several others were witnesses to
an automobile accident in which one car was totally demolished, and the other car merely damaged. Now, one witness
might report, "I just saw a wreck, and a car was totally

demolished!" Someone else who saw the same wreck might exclaim, "I just observed a wreck and two cars were damaged!" They are both right, and such is likely the case in Bartimaeus's experience.

The purpose of this chapter is not to defend the Bible. We don't have to do that. Charles Haddon Spurgeon wrote, "There is no need to defend a lion when he is being attacked. All we have to do is open the gate and let him out. He will defend himself!"

I am convinced that people today are hungry to hear, "What saith the Word of God?" Certainly this explains why a common characteristic of growing, soul-winning churches is an insistent belief in the total trustworthiness of the Word of the living God.

Let's open the gate and let the Bible speak for itself. Note first:

The Defined Extent of an Inspired Bible

All scripture . . . (2 Tim. 3:16*a*).

That little word *all* is very inclusive! It means exactly that. The Bible says, "The law of the Lord is perfect" (Ps. 19:17). The Bible further says, "Every word of God is pure" (Prov. 30:5). There are those who comment, "I believe part of the Bible but not all of the Bible." Some say the Bible *contains* the Word of God, but that it is not *the* Word of God. But the Bible speaks for itself: "ALL SCRIPTURE is given by inspiration of God" (author's caps).

There may be different degrees of *worth* in the Scriptures, but there are not different degrees of *inspiration*. All Scripture is *equally inspired*. For example, one might receive more *worth* reading the Sermon on the Mount (Matt. 5—7) than from reading the genealogy found in Matthew's first chapter. But one is just as inspired as the other. This is the defined extent of the inspired Bible—ALL SCRIPTURE.

I am well aware that there are several different views of

inspiration. There are those who adhere to *dynamic inspiration*. Dynamic inspiration holds the position that God inspired the Bible in ways mankind cannot understand and through unidentifiable processes, and that God sharpened the natural abilities of man to write lucidly. This view is not dependent on spelling out the process by which God inspired the Bible. Some accept what is referred to as *moral inspiration*, believing that the Bible is inspired and reliable only in moral or spiritual matters, but not necessarily in scientific, historical, or genealogical matters. Others believe in what I would call *thought inspiration*, which indicates that God gives the thoughts, allowing men to write them down in their own words. Actually, these three approaches overlap.

My own view is called *plenary verbal*. God inspired the words. Men, under the power of the Holy Spirit, wrote them down.

Jesus declared, "Think not that I am come to destroy the law, or the prophets: I am not come to destroy, but to fulfil. For verily I say unto you, Till heaven and earth pass, one jot or one tittle shall in no wise pass from the law, till all be fulfilled" (Matt. 5:17-18).

Now, a jot is the smallest character in the Hebrew alphabet. A tittle is smaller than a comma and is used in Hebrew to distinguish consonants. This is illustrated in our English alphabet by the dot of an *i* and the cross of a *t*. Jesus taught that not a jot—the dot of an *i*—or a tittle—the cross of a *t*—shall pass away from this holy, inspired Book.

In determining what to believe regarding any certain matter, it is imperative that we view Jesus as the perfect example. What did Jesus have to say about the Bible? Ironically, one of the places where we gain the keenest insights into his belief in the Word of God was during the temptation after Jesus' fasting in the wilderness. Matthew 4 reveals some important truths about Jesus' own view concerning the Bible. He had been fasting for forty days when the devil came with the first temptation, saying, "See these stones? If you are really the Son of God, command these stones to be made bread." Jesus replied, "It is written, Man shall not live by bread alone, but by EVERY WORD THAT PROCEEDETH OUT OF THE MOUTH OF GOD" (Matt. 4:4, author's caps). Jesus said not *some* words but *every* word. Jesus believed that "all scripture is given by inspiration of God."

The second temptation presents the revealing insight. The devil now took Jesus to the pinnacle of the Temple and told him that, if he were really the Son of God, he could jump off and be rescued. Satan, misquoting Psalm 91:11-12 in this temptation, said, "For he shall give his angels charge over thee. They shall bear thee up in their hands, lest thou dash thy foot against a stone." Satan subtly omitted the middle of the verse which says, "to keep thee in all thy ways." By this omission he distorted the whole promise of the Word of God—that God will preserve the righteous but not when they take stupid risks. This is what Satan was trying to get Jesus to do—to take an unnecessary risk. The Lord Jesus responded by saying, in essence, that to rest his case on part of a verse would be to tempt the Lord God. Instead Jesus relied on *every word*, including every word in Psalm 91:11-12. Jesus, of course, believed that every word of God was true and trustworthy. That's enough for me.

So, Jesus believed all Scripture was God's completely true Word. Let's briefly examine what he personally thought of several matters which concern us today. Some claim that Moses did not write the Pentateuch, the first five books of the Old Testament. What did Jesus say? In John 5:46 he said, "For had ye believed Moses, ye would have believed me: for he wrote of me." In John 7:19 he asked a question, "Did not Moses give you the law?" Concerning Jesus' road to Emmaus walk with the two disciples, the Scriptures record, "And beginning at Moses and all the prophets, he expounded unto them in all the scriptures concerning himself" (Luke 24:27).

Jesus left no doubt as to his belief in the Mosaic authorship of the Pentateuch.

Some have contended that Adam and Eve were not historical figures, but rather were merely representations or symbolizations of mankind itself. Jesus said in Matthew 19:4, "Have ye not read, that he which made them at the beginning made them male and female . . .?"

Some say there wasn't a flood which destroyed the earth in the days of Noah. What did Jesus believe? "As the days of Noe were, so shall also the coming of the Son of man be. For as in the days that were before the flood they were eating and drinking, marrying and giving in marriage, until the day that Noe entered into the ark, And knew not until the flood came, and took them all away; so shall the coming of the Son of man be" (Matt. 24:37-39). Jesus believed the Genesis Flood was a past historical account.

Still others say that Jonah's being swallowed by the fish (*whale* in the King James Version, Matt. 12:40) is nothing more than a fairy tale or at the most an allegory. What did Jesus believe? "For as Jonas was three days and three nights in the whale's belly; so shall the Son of man be three days and three nights in the heart of the earth." Jesus plainly believed the historical authenticity of Jonah.

So, I feel that the real issue is more complex than a simple undermining of the authority of the Word of God. To me, it appears that at times there is a subtle attack on the veracity of Jesus Christ. Jesus believed in the historicity of Adam and Eve, the Mosaic authorship of the Pentateuch, the fish's swallowing of Jonah, and the inspiration of the Scriptures.

The defined extent of an inspired Bible, simply stated, is found in the first two words of the text: "All scripture is given by inspiration of God." Jesus believed in the Scriptures of the Old Testament—of course, when he ministered on earth the New Testament had not been written. And he certainly believed in the inspiration of the New Testament writings because they were written to testify of him. Jesus believed in inspiration. Peter, Paul, and the apostles also believed in inspiration. And that's what I choose to believe. That is: not some, not part, not most, but all—every jot and tittle. *All scripture.* This is its defined extent. Second, I note:

The Detailed Evidence of an Inspired Bible

. . . is given by inspiration of God (2 Tim. 3:16*b*).

The Scripture is "given." It is supernatural. It is given by God. It originates with God, not with man! The detailed evidence of this fact is found in the Bible's unique nature. The Bible is not really a book. It is a library of sixty-six books written over the course of over 1,400 years by at least forty different authors from all walks of life. Some were fishermen, others prophets, kings, shepherds, doctors, or rabbis. What's more, the books were written in different parts of the Mediterranean world of that day. Yet, the Bible has come together with one theology, one plan of redemption, and one theme running throughout its pages, leaving no explanation for its unique nature outside of God himself. It is "given by inspiration of God," which is part and parcel of its detailed evidence.

It is also evidenced by the way in which it can change a person's life. Millions of persons across the world can attest today that the Christ, alive in them, was quickened and made known as he was revealed to them from the written Word. Jeremiah said it well: "Thy words were found and I did eat them; and thy word was unto me the joy and rejoicing of mine heart" (Jer. 15:16).

Surely one of the greatest proofs that the Bible is indeed the Word of God is the manner in which prophecy is fulfilled throughout its pages. For example, we read in the Book of Isaiah, written 700 years before the incarnation of our Lord Jesus, that the promised Messiah would be born of a virgin. Micah prophesied 500 years before Jesus' birth that He would be born in the little town of Bethlehem. Even to this very day the prophetic writings of Ezekiel and scores of other prophecies are being fulfilled before our eyes. The Bible has never yet been wrong—and it never will be! Fulfilled prophecy is convincing evidence that it is the living Word of God.

The Bible says, "All scripture is *given by inspiration of God*" (author's italics). In the original language that phrase is one word, *theopneustos.* It is the result of the breath of God. It literally means "God-breathed." God used men, but he did not breathe on men—he breathed out of men. He breathed out of them the Word of God! As a skilled musical composer creates a score utilizing the flute, the trumpet, and other instruments, so God chose his own instruments. Some were as different as flutes and trumpets. Yet, he chose them and used them to breathe out through them his Word.

This was not mechanical dictation. The Bible writers were not mere stenographers having their minds in neutral and playing the part of nothing more than puppets. Not at all! In fact, I know of no reputable conservative scholar who believes such. This, however, is often the accusation of those who question the true conservative viewpoint. The writers' individual personalities and styles obviously appear in the Word of God, but God was in control. Yet, God controlled them in their writing. God was behind their heredity, their environment, their salvation, their call, and everything about their lives.

Inspiration means that the words are God's words, but he chose to deliver them through men. Second Peter 1:21 states, "Holy men of God spake as they were moved by the Holy Ghost." The meaning here is aptly illustrated in the account of Paul's shipwreck found in Acts 27, where Paul, then a prisoner, was en route to Rome aboard ship. There arose a fierce storm and the sailors, no longer able to guide the ship because of the strong winds, let the wind take the ship wherever the wind blew. Finally, the ship wrecked at Malta.

That account in Acts records these words, "When the ship was caught, and could not bear up into the wind, we let her drive" (Acts 27:15). The word in this account used to describe the ship being driven by the wind is the same one used in 2 Peter 1:21, which says that holy men of God spoke as they were *moved* by the Holy Spirit. Just as the sailors were active in the ship, even though they had no control over where it went, so were the Bible writers. In a very real sense, the writings were not their own. The same Greek word is used in both accounts. God expressed it in Jeremiah 1:9 when he said: "I have put my words in thy mouth." The writers of the Bible did not give us the Scriptures—God did, using those writers as his instruments.

Note carefully the words, "All scripture is given by inspiration." The writings are inspired. God did not breathe on the words of men—God breathed out the words himself! This is what 2 Timothy 3:16 means. Yes, God breathed and Moses wrote it down. God breathed and David wrote it down. God breathed and Isaiah wrote it down. God breathed and John wrote it down.

Every word of the Bible points to Jesus! It is the Jesus Book. Jesus himself emphasized that verity. In John 5:39-40, as he chided the scribes and Pharisees, Jesus nevertheless laid before them the truth that the Scriptures testify of him. "Search the scriptures; for in them ye think ye have eternal life: and they are they which testify of me. And ye will not come to me, that ye might have life." Luke reported, "And beginning at Moses and all the prophets, he expounded unto them in all the scriptures the things concerning himself" (Luke 24:27).

The detailed evidence of an inspired Bible is found in the fact that it is supernatural—it is given by God. It is not the mere writing of man. The Word did not originate with men. It originated with God! "All scripture is *given by inspiration of God.*" Third of all, we see:

The Divine Effect of an Inspired Bible

. . . and is profitable for doctrine, for reproof, for correction, for instruction in righteousness . . . (2 Tim. 3:16*c*).

The divine effect of an inspired Bible is: it is *profitable*. I once heard John MacArthur relate the story of a lady who lived way out in the country. It seems that one day a vacuum cleaner salesman was calling on homes along a country road. He stopped at the lady's home, knocked on her door, and immediately began a high-pressure sales talk. "Ma'am, this is the greatest product on the market. It will suck up anything and everything. The truth is if I don't control it real good, it will suck up the carpet right out from under me."

Before the lady could say a word he continued, "Lady, I want to give you a demonstration." He stepped into her home, went immediately to the fireplace, scooped up several ashes from the fireplace, and deposited them in the middle of the rug, making a large mess. "Ma'am, I *guarantee* this will suck up every spot I put on your rug." The lady stood speechless. "And, lady, if it doesn't I personally will eat it all up with a spoon!" "Well, sir," she replied, "start eating because we ain't got no electricity out here!"

We sometimes find ourselves in positions where our products will not work. But that never happens with the Bible. It is profitable. This is its divine effect.

One might ask "profitable for what?" To begin with, it is profitable for "doctrine," teaching us what we never would have known otherwise. It acquaints us with our fallen condition and God's plan of redemption. Everything we need to know about doctrine is laid down for us in the Word of God. It is also profitable for reproof. When we sin, the Bible convicts us. Jeremiah 23:29 says, "Is not my word like as a fire? saith the Lord; and like a hammer that breaketh the rock in pieces?" The Bible says that its effect is like a hammer which continues to beat us with conviction and reproves us of

our sin. The Bible is also profitable for correction. When we
stray from the straight path, it corrects us, showing the way
back into fellowship with God. It is also profitable for instruction, training us in the way we should go and grow.

We see the proof of this profitable statement found in the
epistles of Paul. In Romans . . . the Bible is profitable for
doctrine. In the letters to the Corinthians . . . the Bible is
profitable for reproof. In Galatians . . . the Bible is profitable
for correction. In the Epistle of Paul to the Ephesians . . . the
Bible is profitable for instruction.

This verse (2 Tim. 3:16) tells us that the Bible is like God's
road map. First, there is *doctrine*, the way we begin the road
with Christ. Here is proper teaching which shows us God's
way. When we obey it and come to Christ, we start on the
road with him. But what happens when we veer along the
road? We see that the Bible is profitable not only for doctrine
but for *reproof*. It reproves us and helps us recognize a wrong
turn.

How does one get straight on the path? Here is where the
Bible is profitable for *correction*. The Word shows us how to go
straight on the road with God. And what happens once we
are going straight once again? The Bible is profitable for
instruction. The Word shows us how to stay on the road so we
will not wander off again! This is the divine effect of an
inspired Bible. It is profitable.

All teachings and all theologies are to be tested by the Word
of God and if contrary, dealt with and rejected. Let's walk
around this point for just a moment—the Bible is indeed
profitable for correction.

*What about those who claim they have inspired books outside the
Bible?* Mormons are among them. They are garnering thousands of new followers across the world, sending out many of
their young missionaries on bicycles. They claim that Joseph
Smith received a revelation, gold plates from God. Smith
allegedly wrote down the inscriptions from the plates, and it

became the *Book of Mormon*. But the Bible says, "For I testify unto every man that heareth the words of the prophecy of this book, If any man shall add unto these things, God shall add unto him the plagues that are written in this book: And if any man shall take away from the words of the book of this prophecy, God shall take away his part out of the book of life, and out of the holy city, and from the things which are written in this book" (Rev. 22:18-19). Yes, the Bible is profitable for correction.

What about those who have false ideas about Jesus Christ? They are many, and Christian Scientists are among them. In their materials they have stated that Jesus Christ is not God, exclaiming that a part of their purpose is to "correct the fallacy that Jesus is God." But the Bible says, "In the beginning was the Word, and the Word was with God, and the Word was God. . . . And the Word was made flesh and dwelt among us . . . (John 1:1,14). Jesus said, "I and my Father are one" (John 10:30). The Bible even says that Jesus' name shall be called "the everlasting Father." "For unto us a child is born, unto us a son is given; and the government shall be upon his shoulder: and his name shall be called Wonderful, Counsellor, The mighty God, *The everlasting Father*, The Prince of Peace" (Isa. 9:6, author's italics). Christian Scientists also claim that the writings of their prophetess, Mary Baker Patterson Glover Eddy, are equally inspired with those of Jesus himself! Read Revelation 22:18-19 again. The Bible is indeed profitable for correction.

What about those who insist on keeping Saturday as the sabbath? They say that Saturday is the day of worship, that it is a part of the moral law instead of being the ceremonial law. What does the Bible say? Listen to the words of John 5:18, "The Jews sought to kill him [Jesus] because he had broken the sabbath." Jesus broke the Jews' concepts of the sabbath. Jesus himself declared that man was not made for the sabbath but that the sabbath was made for man.

The truth of the Scriptures is that the sabbath was only for the Jews under ceremonial law and for no one else. It was a specific covenant sign between God and them. Adam didn't keep a sabbath. Neither did Abraham. Nor Isaac. Nor Jacob. And in the New Testament you won't find one word about a Christian being commanded to keep the sabbath. Many people refer to Sunday as the sabbath, but this is far from being biblically correct. Sunday is the Lord's Day, the Christian day of worship and rest (Acts 20:7). Saturday, I repeat, is the sabbath. If we would simply turn to the Bible, it would be profitable for correction.

What about those who insist we must be baptized in water to be saved? Many adhere to what is called baptismal regeneration. They teach that one who is not baptized in water is lost and damned for eternity. Nothing could be farther from the pure truth of the Word of God. What does the Bible say? "He that believeth and is baptized shall be saved: He that believeth not shall be damned" (Mark 16:16). Note what it is that damns a person. The Scriptures do not say it is because one is not baptized in water, but because one has not believed on the Lord Jesus Christ. Again the Bible is profitable for correction.

What about our friends who have been indoctrinated since childhood with the unbiblical view that we approach God in prayer through Mary and the saints? What does the Bible say? "For there is one God, and one mediator between God and men, the man Christ Jesus" (1 Tim. 2:5). Yes, the Bible is profitable for correction.

What about the Jehovah's Witnesses who believe, among other unbiblical teachings, that there was no bodily resurrection of our Lord Jesus Christ? They teach that he did not, in fact, return from the grave in bodily form. But the Bible records that Jesus himself said upon appearing to the disciples in his resurrected body in an upper room, "Behold my hands and my feet, that it is I myself." The Witnesses also deny belief in the biblical doctrine of hell, claiming there is no such place, that it means annihilation. But the Bible reveals quite the contrary. In fact, Jesus taught more about hell than he did about heaven. Jesus warned us about going to such a horrible, dreadful place. In describing the sheep-goat judgment in Matthew 25, Jesus indicated he would say to the lost in that day, "Depart from me, ye cursed, into everlasting fire, prepared for the devil and his angels."

The Witnesses, along with many other groups, also teach that salvation is to be earned by good works. But the Bible says, "For by grace are ye saved through faith; and that not of yourselves; it is the gift of God: Not of works, lest any man should boast" (Eph. 2:8-9). Thank God for the Bible! It is profitable for correction.

Not only is it profitable for doctrine, reproof, and correction, it is also profitable for instruction or training in righteousness.

An effective ministry of God's Word will do all four—teach doctrine, reprove sin, correct false paths, and instruct in righteousness. Some churches today have gone to seed on doctrine to the virtual exclusion of reproof, correction, and instruction in righteousness. These groups are dying because of their emphasis on doctrine alone. Others have gone to seed on reproof and seldom, if ever, teach doctrine or instruct in righteousness. Their main concern lies in how long a man's hair is and how short a woman's dress is. Another group has gone to seed on correction while excluding doctrine, reproof, and instruction in righteousness. Like those gone to seed on reproof, they are so polemic that they think God has called them to correct everyone else while the lost world sits by watching and goes quietly to hell.

Still others have gone to seed on instruction in righteousness. This constant emphasis on righteousness and the deeper life, without any strong teaching on doctrine, reproof, and correction, has led to more than one division in a local body of believers. An effective ministry of the Word of God will be a balanced ministry of the Word of God—and will teach doctrine, reprove sin, correct false paths, and instruct in righteousness.

The church that stands on the trustworthiness of the Word of God is one that God blesses because the Bible is profitable. This is why liberal denominations have shriveling memberships, struggle to meet their budgets, have no real joy, and few people are converted and added to their rolls. It is a supernatural principle; God will not invest many new converts in a ministry that will not teach them the Word of God, reprove them of their sin, correct them in the right path, and instruct them in righteousness through the Word of God. This is why the growing churches today, the churches which are reaching great numbers of people for Jesus, insist that the Bible is *truth, without any mixture of error.* It is not enough that we simply talk evangelism and missions. They must be rooted and grounded in the Bible which is totally inspired by God in its content. The divine effect of an inspired Bible is: it is profitable. It works! Finally, let us note:

The Desired End of an Inspired Bible

That the man of God may be perfect, throughly furnished unto all good works (2 Tim. 3:17).

And what is the desired end of a totally inspired Bible? First of all, that the man of God might be perfect [complete], that his life might be whole. The truth is, we cannot be what God intends us to be without the Word of God. The desired end of the Word of God is that we might be complete. Note once again what Jeremiah found when he fed upon the Word of God: "Thy words were found and I did eat them and they became the joy and rejoicing of my heart" (Jer. 15:16). True joy and rejoicing only come when we are made complete through the truth of the Word. It has been observed, "A Bible that is falling apart usually belongs to someone who isn't!"

And, once we are complete, we are "throughly furnished

unto all good works." Being made complete has to do with our *life*. And getting equipped for all good works has to do with our *service*. Once we are complete, *then* we are equipped. God doesn't call the equipped—he equips the called. Note the order. First one's life, and then one's service. This is the principle upon which we are seeking to build a New Testament church in Fort Lauderdale. We call it *being comes before doing*. Being comes before doing because what we do will always be determined by who and what we are. When we are complete in Christ, then our good works will be supernaturally natural and naturally supernatural. Being does not eliminate doing. Being accelerates doing!

This is the desired end of an inspired Bible—that you might be complete, in order to be equipped, in order to live for God, in order to give him glory and honor in so doing. The Bible is the inspired Word of God. The Bible is all truth. It is fact and not fiction. Look at its *defined extent*: "All scripture." Recall its *detailed evidence*: "is given by inspiration of God." Its *divine effect*? It is "profitable for doctrine, for reproof, for correction, for instruction in righteousness." And its *desired end* is "that the man of God may be perfect [complete], throughly furnished unto all good works."

A few years ago, my wife Susie and I were returning from Israel and stayed overnight in Paris, France. Since we don't have an opportunity to be in Paris every weekend, we naturally wanted to cram as much as possible into our afternoon and evening. Susie and the others in our party insisted upon going to the Louvre, the world-renowned Paris art gallery. Now, to be quite honest, I could think of nothing I would least like doing than spending my one Parisian afternoon in an art gallery!

We voted, I lost, and off to the Louvre we went. I must admit it was a most impressive museum with room after room and corridor after corridor filled with the great paintings of the world. After an hour or two we went into a particularly large room. I looked toward the end of the room. There was a painting protected by armed guards who stood on either side. A large crowd had gathered around it. We walked down to investigate. And there before our very eyes was the original Mona Lisa!

I remembered a story I had heard a preacher tell about that painting, and my first reaction was much like his: "So that's the famous Mona Lisa I have heard so much about all my life. That thing? I really don't understand what's so unusual about it." And then I began to think: *the issue is not what I think about the Mona Lisa at all.*

You see, when we view the Mona Lisa it's not on trial—we are. Our aesthetic values and our appreciation of art are on trial. The Mona Lisa has withstood the test of time. It will still be one of the famous paintings when most of the paintings of the world have passed into obscurity. We are on trial—not the Mona Lisa.

And reader, when we view the precious Word of God, it is not on trial—we are. It has withstood the test of time. It is still to this day the best-seller in the world. It will still be the Book of books when all other writings of men have faded into oblivion. And when we reach the judgment bar of God, our lives had best measure up to the teachings of this inspired and living Word.

2.
What About the Poor?

Blessed are the merciful: for they shall obtain mercy (Matt. 5:7).

This chapter cannot be avoided by any local expression of the body of Christ. The church can no longer remain silent on the issue of the poor while hoping federal government programs will continue to relieve her guilt. Nearly every government welfare program is an indictment of the church's neglect to remember the poor. It is strange that, by and large, we have virtually ignored the very people with whom Jesus spent his ministry while we retreat within our stained-glass walls to sing our pious hymns about becoming "more like the Master."

This is the day of the open door for the church which takes seriously the command of Jesus to carry the gospel to the poor and begins to go after the type of people no other church seems to want. In our churches on Sunday morning, there are too few of the kind of folks to whom Jesus devoted most of his ministry.

The Beatitudes of our Lord do not comprise a set of rules by which we are to live, but instead a convincing picture of the life which each of his followers should lead. The pathway is plain. First, we are to recognize our poverty of spirit. We are nothing without Christ. Once this is accomplished, then we mourn over our spiritual neglect. This brings us to the place of meekness or surrender to our Master. Then, and only then, can we "hunger and thirst after righteousness" and be filled. And what is the result of being controlled by the Spirit of

God? The first mark is that we will be "merciful." Show me a person being controlled by the Spirit of God, and I'll show you someone who shows mercy to others. On the other hand, show me someone who does not demonstrate mercy, and you'll see someone who is not being controlled by the Spirit of God.

In the Sermon on the Mount, Jesus was saying to that self-righteous, selfish crowd, "what really matters is on the inside." The matter of showing mercy is a good barometer of what is on the inside. This is why our Lord is revealed in the Gospels as continually ministering to the poor.

We sing, "More Like the Master." If we really mean it and we are truly like Jesus, we will be about the business of seeking to save the lost by taking the gospel to the poor.

What about the poor? In light of the Scriptures, the plight of the poor is a question that no body of believers can avoid. Jesus addressed this question in Matthew 5:7 by giving *a pronounced blessing* and *a promised benefit*.

A Pronounced Blessing

Blessed are the merciful

What does it mean to be merciful? It is not merely a humanistic idea that if we are good to others, they will be good to us. This simply is not true. Jesus was the most merciful man who ever lived. He reached out to the sick and healed them, to the crippled and gave them new legs, to despised tax collectors, prostitutes, and outcasts and drew them into his circle of love. He called the lonely and made them feel loved.

What was the response of the "religious" people of the day? They scoffed, "Look who he's always with. The scum, the despised, the riffraff of society." I suppose those Pharisees will always be with us. They are certainly around today. Jesus was the most merciful man who ever lived, and yet they screamed for his blood.

What did our Lord mean when he said, "Blessed are the merciful"? I am convinced he was speaking of our relationship with one another—"Be merciful to others and God will be merciful to you." Mercy is seeing a kid at school just wishing someone would speak to him, and showing that kid some attention. Mercy is seeing a person in need of real *agape* love and taking the time to give that love. Mercy is seeing a lonely person and sharing comfort. Mercy is meeting a need, not simply feeling it!

Why aren't more of us who are followers of the Lord Jesus showing mercy to others? Is it because we are too good? Is it because we are too busy? Is it because we are too afraid? Or is it because we are too phony?

Jesus was the embodiment of mercy. Remember, we are supposed to be like him. For thirty-three years the world saw a picture of what the body of Christ ought to be. Jesus walked, he talked, he lived among us, and shared his life with us. Today those of us who are believers make up the visible body of Christ on Planet Earth. I fear that in too many places we are giving the world a puny picture of our Lord Jesus. If we are to give the right picture of Jesus to the world, we need to be like him.

Jesus Christ had a special relationship with the poor. He was born in the most impoverished circumstances imaginable. This King of kings, this Lord of lords, was not born in a palace, not even a hospital, not even a hotel, not even in the common decency of a clean room. He came into this world in the most destitute conditions imaginable—a cave filled with animals where sickness, disease, and death all were likely possibilities. We try to beautify the stable in Bethlehem, but the truth is: in the filth and the dung our Lord came into this world.

Yes, Jesus had a special relationship with the poor. When Mary and Joseph presented him as a baby at his dedication in the Temple, they could afford only two turtle doves as a sacrifice. Thirty years later when Jesus stepped out of the carpenter shop, walked across the dusty street of Nazareth, and stood up to preach his first sermon in the synagogue, his first words were, "The Spirit of the Lord God is upon me, because he hath anointed me to preach the gospel to the poor" (Luke 4:18).

Another interesting insight into Jesus' relationship with the poor occurred when John the Baptist was imprisoned. He sent his disciples to ask our Lord if he were really the Messiah or should they look for another. Do you remember Jesus' reply? Jesus told the disciples of John to go back and tell John that "the poor have the gospel preached unto them."

Jesus had a special relationship with the poor throughout his life. In fact, he even died in poverty. He was buried in poverty. He did not even have a tomb in which to be placed and was buried in a borrowed tomb. Many of his earliest followers were poor. Do you remember the reply of Peter and John to the beggar at the Beautiful Gate of the Temple in Acts 3:6? They declared, "Silver and gold have I none; but such as I have give I thee."

This relationship of Jesus to the poor continued after the ascension. Paul the apostle relates in Galatians 2 his journey to Jerusalem seventeen years after the Damascus road experience. There he met with Peter and the other disciples. They concluded that Peter would stay in Jerusalem and carry the gospel to the Jews and that Paul and Barnabas would leave and share the gospel with the Gentile world. Then Paul makes an incredible statement, saying, "All they asked was that I remember the poor" (see v. 10). As he left Jerusalem to further the gospel to the world, the thought on the mind of all of the apostles was to "remember the poor." And "preach the gospel to the poor."

Now, we say we are followers of Jesus. We go through our little worship rituals every week, singing about how much we love him and how much we follow him. The real question is, to whom have you shown mercy this week? It's no wonder so few of us are living abundant, happy lives. Jesus said, "Blessed [happy] are the merciful."

The truth is, the poor are not going to go away. Jesus said, "The poor you have with you always" (Matt. 26:11, NASB). That certainly blows a hole in the Communists' propaganda, doesn't it? Communism is obviously not the answer. The poor will always be with us. What are we, the church of the Lord Jesus Christ, going to do about it? Are we going to take seriously this command of Jesus to "remember the poor" or are we going to hope that federal government programs will continue to come through so we will not look so bad in the eyes of our community?

If we are really like Jesus, we'll begin to show mercy to the poor. The world is full of people who are hurting, lonely, defeated, hungry, uneducated, poor. Isn't it strange how so many churches isolate themselves from the very people with whom Jesus spent most of his time?

Barry was a sight to behold when he dragged up to our church one Sunday morning. His eyes were red from lack of sleep, his body bent from the weight of the large backpack he was carrying, and he was hungry. One of our ushers spotted him out front and gave him a warm welcome, a doughnut, and a hot cup of coffee. Barry couldn't believe that a well-dressed, Gentile Baptist could care anything about a down-and-out Jewish boy on the run!

Drawn by this unconditional love and acceptance, Barry decided to stay for church to see why this man would care so much. The love of Jesus began constraining Barry. After church some of our singles found Barry a place to stay. He began coming to the services and reading the Bible. He soon learned that we Baptists were not asking him to convert to our religion. The truth is, in a sense, we had converted to his! The

Lord Jesus is indeed the promised Messiah. Barry received Jesus as his own personal Savior, and he is still growing taller in the faith with each passing month.

Barry is part of God's family today because an usher at a high-steepled, downtown church cared enough to walk across the street to say welcome. Folks "love the unlovely" and take seriously the commandment of Jesus to share the gospel to the poor when they are being controlled by God's Spirit.

The more we become like Jesus, the more we will show mercy on the poor and the rejects of society. Jesus loves the rejects of society. After all, who led the children of Israel through the Red Sea? A society reject. A slave, a murderer, named Moses. Who slew Goliath? A reject. A ruddy-faced shepherd boy who was the least son of Jesse of Bethlehem. His name was David. Who started the Methodists? A reject from society, John Wesley had no pulpit in which to preach so he preached in the streets. Who wrote *The Pilgrim's Progress*? A reject, John Bunyan, who was in prison. Who wrote the Book of Philippians? A reject, Paul who was a prisoner in Rome. Who wrote the Gospel of John and the Book of the Revelation? A reject, John, who, as an old man, was exiled to the Isle of Patmos.

God in his wisdom and mercy uses the rejects. Jesus loves the rejects. The only institution in the world which goes door to door seeking a bunch of poverty-stricken people whom the world says will be liabilities instead of assets is the New Testament church. General William Booth, the founder of the Salvation Army, said, "When you go to the poor with the gospel, the rich join hands with you to take it there." Our church sends out four hundred trained lay evangelists each week. Why? To bring back the rejects. Jesus loves the rejects!

When Jesus went to Jerusalem, where did he go? He went to the pool of Bethesda. There a large group of impotent people were lying. He went to the rejects. He went to a man

who had been lame for thirty-eight years. When our Lord
went to Jericho, where did he go? Did he make a beeline for
the city hall to meet the mayor? No, he went to the wayside
where the blind beggar, Bartimaeus, was rattling his tin cup.
When our Lord went to Sychar, where did he go? Did he
make a mad dash to meet the governor of Samaria? No, he
went to an out-of-the-way place and had a conversation with a
reject, a prostitute, and told her of living water. When our
Lord died, he died with two rejects, and took one of them by
the hand into heaven.

Strange, isn't it, how so many churches today have isolated
themselves from the very people with whom Jesus spent his
whole ministry. He taught, "Blessed are the merciful."

A new day dawned in our church at Fort Lauderdale when
we decided that we were going after people no other church
seemed to want. The words of Jesus pierced our hearts when
he said, "When thou makest a dinner or a supper, call not thy
friends, nor thy brethren, neither thy kinsman, nor thy rich
neighbors; lest they also bid thee again, and a recompence be
made thee. But when thou makest a feast, call the poor; the
maimed, the lame, the blind: And thou shalt be blessed; for
they cannot recompense thee; for thou shalt be recompensed
at the resurrection of the just" (Luke 14:12-14).

A few years ago we decided to act on the words of Jesus.
Every year now on the Saturday before Thanksgiving, we
have our annual "Feast of Plenty" where everyone in our city
is invited to share a huge full-course turkey dinner and
thanksgiving meal. We spread tables on our parking lot to
feed the five thousand, and the ministry continues through
the year in our various ministries to the poor. Believe me,
none of us has been the same since we accepted at face value
the commandment of Jesus to carry the gospel to the poor.

Jesus said: "For I was an hungered, and ye gave me no
meat; I was thirsty and ye gave me no drink; I was a stranger,
and ye took me not in; naked, and ye clothed me not; sick,

and in prison, and ye visited me not. Then shall they also answer him, saying, Lord, when saw we thee an hungered, or athirst, or a stranger, or naked, or sick, or in prison and did not minister unto thee? Then shall he answer them, saying, Verily I say unto you, inasmuch as ye did it not to one of the least of these, ye did it not to me. And these shall go away into everlasting punishment; but the righteous into life eternal" (Matt. 25:42-46). We believe that as our church serves multiplied thousands of people during the year, we are actually ministering unto Jesus himself. While the Matthew passage relates to a coming day, Jesus is, in a sense, coming by every day in the face of an unshaven man, in the bent body of an old woman, in the anguished, dirty face of a little child. Yes, "Blessed are the merciful!"

The church that neglects the poor has robbed itself of a great blessing from God. If we are to be like Jesus, we will take the *gospel* to the poor. I am convinced that this is the real key. There are a world of social ministries that have sprung up today which are solely humanistic. Our command from Jesus is to take the *gospel* to the poor. Too many people try to pacify their own feelings of not fulfilling this commission with humanistic social ministries.

They go out and find the prodigal son in the pigpen. Then they gather a group together to build a shelter over him; they go to the clothing closet to put some clothes on his back, and they even take him a hot meal on wheels every day. But they leave him in the pigpen! Our task is to give the gospel to the poor. This is what our Lord did in every case. Our commission is to pick up that boy from the pigpen and carry him back to the Father's house. It is interesting that once there, his Father supplied all his needs according to his own riches (see Phil. 4:19).

Let's stop being so hypocritical as we sit piously behind our stained-glass walls talking about how much we care for missions in blackest Africa while we are uncomfortable sitting next to a Haitian refugee in church. Let's stop being so hypocritical as we come to a mission meeting and learn about our work in South America if we do not love the Cuban refugees or the Mexican Americans. If we are going to love the world, we must begin by loving our own world. It is difficult to try and love your neighbor if you do not even know his name. Jesus said there was a pronounced blessing upon those who would take the gospel to the poor—"Blessed are the merciful."

A Promised Benefit
For they shall obtain mercy

Here is a beautiful idea. Do you see the cycle? God gives us mercy, and we are merciful, and God gives us more mercy. The one who has received mercy will be merciful. The one who has received forgiveness will be forgiving. The one who has received love will be loving. Many expose their own phoniness by not being merciful, forgiving, and loving. The reason it is so hard for some people to forgive is: it's been a long time since they've been forgiven.

The truth of the Scriptures is that we always reap what we sow. "Be not deceived; God is not mocked: for whatsoever a man soweth, that shall he also reap" (Gal. 6:7). Jesus said it this way, "Blessed are the merciful: for they shall obtain mercy." What a promised benefit we have from our Lord Jesus. Did you know there are over four hundred promises in the Bible concerning those who minister to the poor?

"Blessed is he that considereth the poor: the Lord will deliver him in time of trouble. The Lord will preserve him, and keep him alive; and he shall be blessed upon the earth; and thou wilt not deliver him unto the will of his enemies. The Lord will strengthen him upon the bed of languishing; thou wilt make all his bed in his sickness" (Ps. 41:1-3). Here is the promise of protection, blessing, and healing for those who remember the poor.

"For he shall stand at the right hand of the poor, to save him from those that condemn his soul" (Ps. 109:31). Where is Jesus Christ? He is not only at the right hand of the Father, he is at the right hand of the poor!

"He that despiseth his neighbor sinneth; but he that hath mercy on the poor, happy is he" (Prov. 14:21). Happy! Have you ever done something for someone and found the joy and happiness it brings?

"He that oppresseth the poor reproacheth his Maker; but he that honoureth him hath mercy on the poor" (Prov. 14:31). Here is a solemn warning about being a reproach to God! When we have mercy on the poor, we are honoring God in the process.

"He that hath pity upon the poor lendeth unto the Lord; and that which he hath given will he pay him again" (Prov. 19:17). What a promise! God pays far better dividends than any savings and loan association around.

"Whoso stoppeth his ears at the cry of the poor, he also shall cry himself, but shall not be heard" (Prov. 21:13). Some of us wonder why our prayers have been unanswered. This may be the very reason!

"Better is the poor that walketh in his uprightness, than he that is perverse in his ways, though he be rich. Whoso keepeth the law is a wise son: but he that is a companion of riotous men shameth his father. He that by usury and unjust gain increaseth his substance, he shall gather it for him that will pity the poor" (Prov. 28:6-8). Strong words. If you do not remember the poor, God will take it from you and give it to those who do!

"He that giveth unto the poor shall not lack; but he that hideth his eyes shall have many a curse" (Prov. 28:27). It may be that the reason some of us are continually failing to make ends meet is because we have absolutely neglected the poor. Jesus said, "Give, and it shall be given unto you; good measure, pressed down, and shaken together, and running over, shall men give into your bosom. For with the same measure that ye mete withal it shall be measured to you again" (Luke 6:38).

"The righteous considereth the cause of the poor; but the wicked regardeth not to know it" (Prov. 29:7). You cannot be right with God and have no concern for the poor. Does it bother you that this year twelve million people will die of starvation before they are five years of age? Does it bother you that today forty thousand people died from starvation around our world? Our kitchen disposals ate better today than two and a half-billion people on our planet.

Our church has not been the same since an unusual visitor happened our way in 1978. He was an unlikely prospect, to say the least, but without a doubt was the most important visitor of the week. With worn, out-of-date clothes, unkempt hair, and unshaven face, he came to the morning service. He happened to sit down by a couple who had been recently converted to Christ. They made him feel welcome and literally wrapped him in arms of Christian love. During the invitation, he came forward as an inquirer regarding this new life about which I had preached. A counselor guided him to the counseling room where the man trusted Christ as his Savior.

Before I left the church that afternoon the old man said, "Sir, I just ate my first meal in four days. A man from the church took me to lunch. Oh Sir, I feel so happy and bubbly on the inside." He then made a strange request: he asked if there were an old broom anywhere around the church. He then spent the afternoon sweeping off the sidewalks and porches of the church where he had met Christ a few hours before. Before he left that evening he gave an offering—the only thing he had to his name, a battered old flashlight. He disappeared as quickly as he had appeared. More often than we realize, we entertain angels unaware when we seriously consider the commandment of Jesus to share the gospel with the poor.

In light of Scripture the question of this chapter must be faced by everyone of us who are called by his name—What about the poor?

3.
D-I-V-O-R-C-E

It hath been said, Whosoever shall put away his wife, let him give her a writing of divorcement: But I say unto you, that whosoever shall put away his wife, saving for the cause of fornication, causeth her to commit adultery; and whosoever shall marry her that is divorced committeth adultery (Matt. 5:31-32).

And said, For this cause shall a man leave father and mother, and shall cleave to his wife: and they twain shall be one flesh? Wherefore they are no more twain, but one flesh. What therefore God hath joined together, let not man put asunder. They say unto him, Why did Moses then command to give a writing of divorcement, and to put her away? He saith unto them, Moses because of the hardness of your hearts suffered you to put away your wives; but from the beginning it was not so. And I say unto you, Whosoever shall put away his wife, except it be for fornication, and shall marry another committeth adultery: and whoso marrieth her which is put away doth commit adultery (Matt. 19:5-9).

To many people divorce is the "unpardonable sin" of our generation, a dead-end street. This delicate issue has a dire need of being addressed, and unfortunately many churches are virtually silent concerning it.

The church today has a tremendous responsibility in speaking forth the word of truth to our young people and children regarding divorce. And there is also a redemptive element through the blood of Christ which must be addressed concerning those who are putting their lives back together again. As we journey through these pages we will simply attempt to make clear the words of Jesus concerning the issue of divorce.

There is a vast difference of opinion among many good and godly people today concerning how divorce is presented in the Scriptures. Some believe that there are absolutely no biblical grounds for divorce, that people must go through life with the mark and stigma upon them to "suffer for righteousness," as some call it. Others believe that adultery is the only biblical grounds permitting divorce (Matt. 5:32; 19:9). Still others would add that desertion is biblical grounds for divorce, according to 1 Corinthians 7.

Part of our problem is that people are merely concerned with what they think and not with what God says. We must avoid the trap of interpreting the Word of God in light of our contemporary culture and situation. We must always interpret our contemporary culture and situation in light of the

Scriptures. Just because our society and culture have changed does not mean that one jot or tittle of the Word of God has changed. I repeat: the real issue is not what we think but what God says!

Why are there so many divorces today? In many areas of our country there are as many divorces filed annually as there are marriages. Why the ever-increasing divorce rate? There are certainly many reasons. One in particular is that this is the first group of young adults who have been reared by modern parents with little discipline in the home. In our situation here in Broward County, Florida, a recent statistic shocked us all. In our county only 7 percent of the households are family units! We are finally seeing the fruit of young adults who have been reared with little or no discipline in the home. Also, there has been a decrease in the place of the Bible in the home. Unfortunately, few fathers spend five minutes a week reading the Word of God to their children. Another major contributing factor to the number of divorces is the departure from biblical teachings concerning husbands, wives, and children. The Word of God speaks rather plainly concerning these matters (see Eph. 5).

Divorce—is it the unpardonable sin? Perhaps some of my readers have gone through divorce in the past. Others are contemplating it now. Still others are not married yet, and some day may face this volatile issue. I am becoming more and more convinced that people today are genuinely interested in "what saith the Lord?" Consequently our task will simply be to make clear the words of Jesus as we note God's perfect intention and God's permissive intervention.

God's Perfect Intention

It hath been said, Whosoever shall put away his wife, let him give her a writing of divorcement (Matt. 5:31).

Too few people really realize the seriousness of divorce in light of God's perfect intention for their lives. God never intended divorce, and he doesn't today! It is always less than his best for you. There are many second marriages better than the first ones, but I believe they are never as good as the first ones could have been!

In examining God's perfect intention, we will note the purpose and the perversion of it. First, the *purpose* of God's perfect intention involves a personal union, a productive union, and a permanent union. Jesus quoted from Genesis 2:24: "For this cause shall a man leave father and mother, and shall cleave to his wife: and they twain shall be one flesh?" (Matt. 19:5). Here was a *personal union*. The Bible records in Genesis 2:22, "And the rib, which the Lord God had taken from man, made he a woman, and brought her unto the man." Here was the first wedding in history. God formed and made the wife just for her husband and then brought her to him, forming a personal union. God formed Adam and then made Eve from his side. He could have made Adam several wives, but he didn't. He didn't create Adam and Eve and Jane. Nor did he create Adam and Eve and Jane and Bob. Why? Because God's perfect intention was a personal union. It is also clear from the Bible that the personal union was to be a heterosexual union. He made Adam and Eve and not Adam and Harold. Originally Adam and Eve were one; for Eve was taken out of Adam.

But note also that God's perfect intention for us is a *productive union*. The Bible says, "For this cause a man shall leave father and his mother, and shall cleave unto his wife and they shall be one flesh." A husband and wife are designed to complete each other. When Adam saw Eve his first words were, "This is now bone of my bones and flesh of my flesh: she shall be called Woman, because she was taken out of Man. Therefore shall a man leave his father and his mother, and shall cleave unto his wife: and they shall be one flesh" (Gen. 2:23-24). The two were to complement each other. I couldn't be me without my wife, Susie. She couldn't be Susie without me. We are opposites in many ways but we complete each other.

God says when he brings two people together they become "one flesh." At the very apex of the marriage act all of one's being, nerves, energies, and the like, become one with the other. Children are a resultant picture of two becoming one flesh. When I look at my daughter, I see my wife and myself in one. God's perfect intention is a productive union—one flesh. The severing of marriage bonds is one reason why divorce is so very painful. It is like butchery because it divides asunder what God has brought together as one.

God's perfect intention also involves a *permanent union*. The Bible says, "Wherefore they are no more twain, but one flesh. What therefore God hath joined together, let not man put asunder" (Matt. 19:6). Did you catch that? What God has joined together. What makes marriage a permanent union? The state? The church? The pastor? No, God does! "What God hath joined together, let not man put asunder." No liberal legislation can change that.

The phrase, "let not man put asunder," is not some catchy slogan used at the end of marriage ceremonies by the preacher. It is a direct Word of God which means that no human authority has any right to tamper with the divine ordinance. "Let not man put asunder." This is what is happening today. Such ideas of incompatibility or mental cruelty being the basis for divorce are men putting asunder marriages. These are man-made grounds and not biblical grounds.

God's perfect intention is a personal union, a productive union, and a permanent union. This is why in the wedding ceremonies I perform I always ask the bride and groom as they place the ring on each other's finger to "promise God in your heart you will keep the vows you've made today forever."

Jesus said, "It hath been said, Whosoever shall put away his wife let him give her a writing of divorcement" (Matt. 5:31). Here he alludes to the *perversion* of God's perfect intention. "It hath been said." Where was this said in the Bible? We find the answer in Deuteronomy 24:1-2: "When a man hath taken a wife, and married her, and it come to pass that she find no favour in his eyes, because he hath found some uncleanness in her: then let him write her a bill of divorcement, and give it in her hand, and send her out of his house. And when she is departed out of his house, she may go and be another man's wife." If God's perfect intention is that of a personal union, a productive union, and a permanent union, then why would divorce be allowed to take place in Deuteronomy 24? Jesus gave us the answer in Matthew 19 when he taught it was "because of the hardness of your hearts" (v. 8). In reality God was leading them back to his original pronouncement.

Now there is a perversion and a misconception here. God did not *command* divorce in Deuteronomy 24. It was a reluctant concession. Why? Because of the hardness of their hearts. God was not winking at a man's harshness, but mercifully arranging for a wife to be divorced rather than be slain because her husband wanted to be free from her. Matthew 19:7-8 records, "They say unto him, Why did Moses then command to give a writing of divorcement, and to put her away? He saith unto them, Moses because of the hardness of your hearts suffered you to put away your wives: but from the beginning it was not so." Now, since death dissolved the marriage, men were simply killing their wives in order to be free of them, thus Deuteronomy 24 was not a command. It was given as a merciful concession because of their hard hearts.

One might rightly ask, "Why was adultery not mentioned here if indeed it is spoken of by Jesus in our text as grounds for divorce?" The answer is obvious. Adultery in the Old Testament was a capital offense, punishable by death. Do you remember the woman taken in adultery who was at the point of being stoned by her accusers? Obviously if it were a capital offense there would be no reason for divorce. In fact, adultery being a capital offense did more than herpes is doing today to keep people out of illicit affairs!

Before the Mosaic Law, men would turn their wives out of the house and they would be at the mercy of the world. Therefore, Deuteronomy 24 was given as a preventative. By obtaining a bill of divorcement, a wife was protected, and in this manner the seriousness of marriage was emphasized. The whole focus of Deuteronomy 24 is to help people understand that marriage is not something one can walk into and out of at will. We see, then, that before Jesus dealt with the issue at hand he addressed the perversion when he noted, "It hath been said."

There is much perversion today in this realm. The most common complaint and reason for divorce I hear is, "I just don't love her (him) anymore." This is a crucial issue, and here I write parenthetically for a moment. How does the church deal with this issue? That is, "I simply don't love him (or her) anymore." Some people have the erroneous idea that love is only associated with emotions. This is nowhere to be found in the Word of God. Love is something you do. For example "For God so loved the world, that he gave" (John 3:16).

In the Bible the love for a husband and wife is paralleled with the love of Christ for the church! This is true in Ephesians, Revelation, and many other parts of the Word of God. In fact, in Revelation 2, we find the perfect illustration for this excuse. Here is the bride (the church at Ephesus) who has fallen out of love with the groom (the Lord Jesus). Do you remember the misconception that was found at the church at Ephesus? Verse 4 says, "Thou hast left thy first love." The misconception is that many people think they have lost their first love. Now, there is a world of difference between saying I lost something and saying I left something. It's easier to admit that you lost something than it is to admit that you left something. Many people who are saying they lost their love for their husband or wife are really indicating they left it.

What should one do when this takes place? There are three ideas that arise right out of Revelation 2:5 which show us the answer. "Remember therefore from where you have fallen, and repent and do the deeds you did at first" (NASB). The first thing to do is to remember. Think about the time you first fell in love. The problem with many is that they still live with an immature kind of love. Suddenly your husband or wife doesn't give you chills anymore so you figure you have fallen out of love with him or her. Someone at the office flirts with you, and you feel, "I'm in love." So you divorce your husband or wife and marry another person, and in a few years the process is repeated. Some women get a lawyer, fall in love with him, and the process in repeated again! The truth is you don't know what love is! Love is something you do. You didn't lose that first love—you left it. *Remember*, where did you leave it?

The next step is to repent. "Remember therefore from where you have fallen, and repent and do the deeds you did at first" (Rev. 2:5, NASB). Repent! That is, go back. Love is a spiritual power, it is the fruit of the Spirit. The more you love God, the more you will love your mate. Repentance is toward God.

Finally, one should renew. "Remember therefore from where you have fallen, and repent and do the deeds you did at first." Do those things you did at first. Start doing the things you did then. Treat your mate like you did when you were "in love." If you do, then you will feel. It is easier to act your way into a new feeling than to feel your way into a new way of acting. You'll become so different your mate will respond to you in a new way! Remember! Repent! Renew!

Dear friend, God's perfect intention is a personal union, a productive union, and a permanent union. Hang in there!

God's grace is sufficient. If God does not have enough grace to help you mend an unhappy relationship, to help you love your wife or husband, then Christ is not the all-sufficient answer to mankind's problems. And we know he is!

In understanding this critical issue it is important not only to see God's perfect intention, but also:

God's Permissive Intervention

> But I say unto you, That whosoever shall put away his wife, saving for the cause of fornication, causeth her to commit adultery: and whosoever shall marry her that is divorced committeth adultery (Matt. 5:32).

As we examine God's permissive intervention, there are some false assumptions. Some say there are no grounds for divorce, period. They claim the "exception clause" which Jesus used in Matthew 5 and 19 is only in the case of incest or homosexuality. This is certainly not the view of the over-whelming majority of conservative scholars concerning the word used in Matthew 5:31 and 19:9. The word *fornication* used in these verses could best be translated in the words of Dr. Joel Gregory of Southwestern Baptist Seminary as "a physical act of sexual impurity." Those who adhere to the view that there are no grounds for divorce, point for example to Mark 10:11. "Whosoever shall put away his wife, and marry another, committeth adultery." But we must take a systematic approach to the Scriptures, putting together all that Jesus said concerning divorce, and this includes Matthew 5 and 19.

The Scriptures must always be interpreted in light of Scripture. Briefer statements should be read in light of fuller ones. If we do not, we open ourselves to all sorts of false assumptions. In fact, this is how cults have their beginnings. If we did not interpret Scripture in the light of other Scripture, we would all have to pluck out our eyes and cut off our hands in view of Jesus' Sermon on the Mount.

To explain away the words of Jesus in Matthew 5:31 and 19:9

regarding divorce is like accepting only one portion of the
Great Commission and forgetting the rest. As you know, the
method of the Great Commission is given to us in Matthew
when Jesus told us to go and make disciples, baptize them,
and teach them. The message of the Great Commission is
given to us in Luke when Jesus tells us that "repentance and
remission of sins should be preached . . . among all nations"
(24:47). And then the measure of it is given to us in Mark's
Gospel when Jesus says we should carry the message to the
ends of the earth. For example, to say that the Great Commission simply means to believe—when Luke's version says it
involves repentance and that remission of sins should be
preached, and Matthew's Gospel says converts should be
baptized and taught the faith—is to speak only a half-truth.

Others claim that desertion is cause for divorce, but this
simply is not biblical. It may sometimes seem like it should
be. But we remember the Bible says, "There is a way that
seemeth right unto a man, but the end thereof are the ways of
death" (Prov. 14:12, 16:25). Folk who hold to this position point
to 1 Corinthians 7:15: "Yet, if the unbelieving one leaves, let
him leave; the brother or the sister is not under bondage in
such cases, but God has called us to peace" (NASB). At an
initial glance this appears to pit the teachings of Paul against
the teachings of Jesus. Many build a case for divorce here, but
Paul is not talking about divorce in this passage, as is evident
in verse 11 when he says, "But and if she depart, let her
remain unmarried, or else be reconciled to her husband: and
let not the husband put away his wife."

If desertion were biblical grounds for divorce, how long
does it take before it goes into effect? One week? One month?
One year? Three years? If desertion could dissolve a marriage, thousands and thousands would take advantage of it!

There are cases which justify a woman leaving her husband
but which do not justify divorce, just as there are instances
which justify children being removed from the custody of

their parents. But the purpose of this message is not to deal with hypothetical systems.

Let's look to Jesus, the final authority. "It hath been said, Whosoever shall put away his wife, let him give her a writing of divorcement: But I say unto you, that whosoever shall put away his wife, *[except]* for the cause of fornication, causeth her to commit adultery" (Matt. 5:31-32). These words of our Lord are too plain to be misunderstood!

"But I say," . . . Jesus was saying, in essence, "here is the intention of the Lawgiver." There is much perversion today on the intention of lawgivers. For example there is more concern today in keeping God out of government than government out of God. This was never the intention of those original lawgivers in the first place. Jesus was getting at that matter here and in this whole section of the Sermon on the Mount. That is, the Pharisees were presenting a false interpretation of the law of God. Now Jesus was saying, "But I say." He was giving them the original intent of the Lawgiver.

Jesus says two things may dissolve a marriage. One is death and the other is adultery. The word used in these contexts means "a physical act of sexual impurity." Here is God's permissive intervention. He permits it. Now, God is not declaring we must divorce. He doesn't command it. God has never commanded anyone to divorce. I personally have never counseled anyone to divorce. But the truth we see here is God's permissive intervention.

In the Old Testament the picture of adultery within a marriage is found in the Book of Hosea where Gomer, the prophet Hosea's wife, had turned to adultery. What did he do? He continued to pursue her with a persistent love in her estranged condition. He continued to plead, "Come back, come back." Divorce on the grounds of adultery is permitted, but it is not required by our Lord.

So far as I can see Jesus taught there is one cause for divorce and that is adultery. The one-flesh link has been broken. The person whose divorce is made on the grounds of adultery is entitled to do so according to the words of Jesus. Consequently, they would also be entitled to remarry. I am not advocating a second marriage here. It may be better than the first, but as already mentioned, it will never be as good as the first could have been. Deuteronomy 24:2 says then the divorced one may "go and be another man's wife."

The real issue here is sin. Sin is defined as "missing the mark." This is not the unpardonable sin. Forgiveness is available where there is real repentance toward God. On the authority of the gospel, I must declare that divorce is *not* the unpardonable sin! It is terrible, but God forbid that anyone feel that one has sinned oneself outside the love of God. If you truly repent, cast yourself on the boundless love, mercy, and grace of God; you can be pardoned, but hear the words of Jesus, "Go, and sin no more" (John 8:11).

The gospel is the good news of the second chance. If I did not believe that a person could be made whole in Jesus, accepted in the beloved as though sin had never occurred, I would get out of the ministry. I would never come to my pulpit again. If I did not believe that "there is therefore now no condemnation to them which are in Christ Jesus, who walk not after the flesh, but after the Spirit" (Rom. 8:1) was the truth I would get out. If I did not believe that "the blood of Jesus Christ his Son cleanseth us from all sin" (1 John 1:7), I would get out. If I did not believe that "though your sins be as scarlet, they shall be white as snow; though they be red like crimson, they shall be as wool" (Isa. 1:18), I would get out. Some claim that our First Baptist Church is nothing but a bunch of adulterers and the like. To that I say: "Thank God!" We want to be a land of beginning again.

There is a hill outside the Damascus Gate in the old city of Jerusalem. Every year as I travel there I have a little ritual on the first night. After dinner and after everyone is settled in their hotel, I step out, and take a taxi down the Mount of

Olives, across the Kidron Valley, and over to the Damascus Gate. I get out at the Damascus Gate and walk up the hill about two blocks to where an old Arab bus station sits. I walk between those buildings in the late hours of the night to the base of a hill. I sit down there and talk to the Lord. The name of that hill? Golgotha, Calvary. There my Lord Jesus shed his blood to redeem me from my sin. There the blood of Jesus Christ was shed and 1 John 1:7 says, "The blood of Christ his Son cleanseth us from all sin."

Our church is not a showcase for saints—it is a hospital for sinners. Before any self-righteous, pharisaical legalists begin to point their long fingers of accusation, I say with our Lord Jesus, "He that is without sin among you, let him first cast a stone" (John 8:7).

You say, "Well, what would Jesus say today concerning this issue of the restoration of the divorced one?" He would say the same thing that he said yesterday. After all, the Bible says, "Jesus Christ the same yesterday, and to-day, and for-ever" (Heb. 13:8). If Jesus were here physically, dealing with men and women in adultery today, he would say the same as he did two thousand years ago, recorded for us in Scripture. He once sat at a well in Samaria and spoke with a woman who had been married five times. He did not condemn her in her sin. He spoke to her of living water that would quench her thirst and satisfy her inner need. Now, did he say that she could never be an effective witness for Christ? Here was a woman who pointed her town to Jesus, and she had been married five times. Did he say she must live with a mark of condemnation on her forever as though it were tattooed on her forehead? Some pharisaical legalists today think Jesus would say something different than he did then. That is, they would condemn her and put her on the shelf to "suffer for righteousness."

What about the woman taken in adultery? Jesus came upon a group of religious people with stones in hand about to crush a woman. He knelt down beside her, wrote some words in the sand, looked up into the faces of her accusers and said, "He that is without sin among you, let him first cast a stone." One by one they walked away. She looked into Jesus' loving face and he asked, "Where are those thine accusers? hath no man condemned thee?" She replied, "No man, Lord." Then Jesus made a remarkable statement, "Neither do I condemn thee, go, and sin no more."

Listen, divorce is wrong! Malachi tells us that "God hateth putting away" or divorce (2:16). The home is the basic structural building block of our society. I agree with John Bisagno in *Love Is Something You Do* that the purpose of God is to hold up a high standard, to do everything we can to keep people from falling off that cliff, but once they go over they'll find an ambulance at the bottom.

What do I do as a pastor? What is our churches' task in this delicate issue? We are to build a wall as strong as we can, as high as we can, and as thick as we can, to keep folks from going off that cliff. We are to preach hard against divorce and speak the word of truth in love. But at the same time, we are to keep plenty of gas in the ambulance at the bottom of the hill.

After preaching on divorce in our church a man came to me and said, "Preacher, one year ago I was divorced. Five months ago I came to this church and found a lot of that gas you talked about in the ambulance at the bottom of the hill. The folks took me in and accepted me, loved me, and prayed with me concerning my wife. She was baptized this morning and we are getting married all over again."

It sounds great to stand on a platform, speaking and teaching about issues. But when you spend your time down on the street level, trying to mend broken lives, it's often an altogether different issue. I for one am sick and tired of a Christian community which falls at the feet of a Christian singer, who by his own admission has slept with dozens of women and has been addicted to dope, and then sings from the platform of almost any Christian meeting house and television program today. I for one am sick of a Christian community which calls a convicted murderer of several innocent people a "trophy of grace." And then, if a person is divorced, this same Christian community puts a label on them and acts as if they had the plague! Now, I am not against saved singers or the converted convict. Thank God, they are both trophies of grace. Also, I am not condoning divorce, but I do stand with our Lord in condemning the legalism which Jesus here is attacking.

What should we do? We should bring it all to Jesus. Many of us have talked with counselors, friends; others of us have kept it within ourselves. What should we do? Bring it all to Jesus. God's perfect intention is a personal union, a productive union, and a permanent union. Anything else is less than God's best for you. But the crystal-clear truth is: not all of us have followed God's perfect intention in our lives. Praise the Lord there is also God's permissive intervention. Some of you are reading these words, hurting and bleeding, saying,

> I wish there were some wonderful place
> Called the Land of Beginning Again!
> Where all our mistakes and all our heartaches
> And all our poor selfish grief
> Could be dropped like a shabby old coat at the door,
> And never be put on again.
>
> —LOUISA FLETCHER TARKINGTON

Thank God, there is such a place at the foot of Calvary's cross.

If you are in need of inner healing, fall on your knees at Jesus' feet in real repentance and hear him say, "Neither do I condemn thee, go, and sin no more." Find a fellowship of believers who have the ambulance ready, if you are in need of mending as you come in genuine repentance, who will say with Jesus, "Neither do *we* condemn thee, go, and sin no more."

4.

Understanding
Our Salvation

Being confident of this very thing, that he which hath begun a good work in you will perform it until the day of Jesus Christ (Phil. 1:6).

It is a heartbreaking fact that in too many cities the local bodies of believers are presenting a very anemic picture of the body of Christ. It isn't that we haven't told our people how to receive Jesus into our lives. The problem may lie in the fact that too few of us have told our people what to do with him once he comes in! I am becoming more and more convinced that the real issue is not revival. It is for us to understand our own salvation and who we are in the Lord Jesus. Once this understanding occurs and we begin to live like children of a King, revival will be as natural as water running downhill.

In the Great Commission Jesus told us to go and "make disciples" (Matt. 27:19, NASB). Disciples, once they are born, are made through proper Bible teaching. The reason many claim they are "getting saved" over and over may be that they have never come to understand salvation in the true biblical sense of being eternally secure in Christ through his finished work on Calvary.

What does it really mean to be saved? Many are recipients of salvation; many use the term openly and repeatedly, but few actually understand what it means and how it is obtained.

Most personal-salvation testimonies we hear go something like this—"I heard the gospel of Jesus Christ . . . then I decided to open my life to him . . . I came to Jesus . . . I gave him my life . . . I received him . . . I repented of my sin . . . I decided to follow Jesus . . . I was saved!" Note the constant use of the perpendicular pronoun as if it all depended upon us. As we examine carefully Philippians 1:6 we find that it is all dependent upon God. Paul said: "For I am confident of this very thing, that He who began a good work in you will perfect it until the day of Christ Jesus" (NASB).

The truth of the matter is that God sought us, found us, began the good work in us, will keep us, will perfect that which concerns us until the day of Christ Jesus. After all, did not the shepherd himself go after the sheep until he found it? I am becoming more and more convinced that when we enter heaven we are going to find out how little we had to do with our own salvation. This is the message of the text and of the gospel, "He which hath begun a good work in you will perform it until the day of Christ Jesus."

Some reading this chapter may be recent converts. Other readers have been walking with Jesus for scores of years. Whatever the case, God wants each of us to understand our own salvation. Consequently, our text reveals two important aspects of salvation: (1) the origin of our salvation and (2) the outcome of our salvation. Initially, in order to understand our salvation we must first examine:

The Origin of Our Salvation

He who began a good work in you (Phil. 1:6a, NASB).

Who began the good work? God! You reply, "I thought I did. I thought I repented. I thought I came to Christ. I thought I took the initiative." No! God did. Just as he took the skins in the Garden of Eden to cover Adam and Eve after they had erroneously tried to cover their own sin with fig leaves, so God takes the initiative in covering our sin today. Many are caught in the trap of trying to cover their own sin. The writer of Proverbs was right on target: "He that covereth his sins shall not prosper; but whoso confesseth and forsaketh them shall have mercy" (28:13). Many try to cover sin by excusing it.

"Well, everyone is doing it!" Others take the approach of minimizing it. "Well, it's not as bad as what other people are doing." Still others laugh it off as merely a vice! It is not to be laughed off; it nailed Jesus to the cross. The truth is, we couldn't cover our sin if we wanted to do so. Jesus said, "Ye will not come to me that ye might have life" (John 5:40).

In examining the origin of our salvation, we see that salvation is *preceded by an undeniable condition*. The undeniable condition of a human is that he is "dead in trespasses and sins" (see Eph. 2:1). If we believe the fall was only a partial fall, then we must also believe that man plays a big part in his salvation. But the Bible records that when man fell into sin in Eden's garden, it was a total fall. Consequently, our undeniable condition is that in and of ourselves we are helpless and hopeless to save ourselves.

In our natural condition we are *unresponsive*. The Bible says, "Wherefore, as by one man sin entered into the world, and death by sin; and so *death passed upon all men*, for that all have sinned" (Rom. 5:12). The truth is that people in their natural state are unresponsive. They are "dead." For death has passed upon all people. We didn't one day, out of the clear blue, decide that we wanted to come to Jesus Christ. The truth is in our lost state we were all unresponsive to the gospel.

Not only is the natural man unresponsive, he is also *unperceptive*. Paul says, "But if our gospel be hid, it is hid to them that are lost: In whom the god of this world hath blinded the minds of them which believe not, lest the light of the glorious gospel of Christ, who is the image of God, should shine unto them" (2 Cor. 4:3-4). Paul also writes, "If God peradventure will give them repentance to the acknowledging of the truth; And that they may recover themselves out of the snare of the devil, who are taken captive by him at his will" . . . (2 Tim. 2:25-26). The natural man is unperceptive. He cannot perceive the truths of God for his mind is blinded to them because of his unbelief.

But note also that he is *unteachable*. The Bible says, "But the natural man receiveth not the things of the Spirit of God; for they are foolishness unto him; neither can he know them, because they are spiritually discerned" (1 Cor. 2:14). The natural man does not receive the things of the Spirit of God— neither can he know them! These words of God are certainly plain. The truth is, in our natural, lost condition we are unresponsive, unperceptive, and even more tragic, we are unteachable.

Note also that the lost person is *unrighteous*. The Bible says, "Behold I was shapen in iniquity, and in sin did my mother conceive me" (Ps. 51:5). "And God saw that the wickedness of man was great in the earth, and that every imagination of the thoughts of his heart was only evil continually" (Gen. 6:5). "All we like sheep have gone astray; we have turned every one to his own way; and the Lord hath laid on him the iniquity of us all" (Isa. 53:6). How obvious it is to us that the natural person is an unrighteous person.

This is man's undeniable condition which precedes salvation. He is unresponsive, unperceptive, unteachable, and unrighteous. He can do nothing in and of himself to bring about the miracle of salvation. After all, can a dead man raise himself? Can a bound man loose himself? Can a blind man give himself sight? Job asked, "Who can bring a clean thing out of an unclean? not one" (Job 14:4). Jeremiah inquired, "Can the Ethiopian change his skin, or the leopard his spots? then may you also do good, that are accustomed to do evil" (Jer. 13:23). Yes, the origin of our salvation is preceded by an undeniable condition.

What one determines is what one chooses. Are we sinners because we sin or do we sin because we are sinners? These significant questions determine our theology of salvation. The clear truth is that we sin because we are sinners. We are fallen people and fallen people do not come to Christ any more than water runs uphill.

The perfect illustration is found in John 11 in the story of Lazarus. Lazarus was dead! Just as there was no glimmer of life in Lazarus without Jesus Christ, so are we dead in our trespasses and sins without any hope or glimmer of life. We are unresponsive, unperceptive, unteachable, and unrighteous. The unsaved person is not sick; he is dead. I have pastored for many years and stood at the open graves of hundreds of people who have slipped over into eternity. One thing I have noticed about dead bodies is that when one is dead physically, one doesn't respond to physical things. One doesn't respond to food, temperature, pain, or feelings. He is dead! And when a man is dead spiritually, he does not respond to spiritual things. This is why the unregenerate person has no desire to read the Bible, pray, fellowship with believers, tithe, or do any of the other things about which we are to be obedient.

What a person without Christ needs is not education, morality, medicine, or religion, but life. The truth is plain. Our salvation is preceded by an undeniable condition.

Jesus said, "Ye will not come to me that ye might have life" (John 5:40). In our natural state, without Christ, we are unresponsive, unperceptive, unteachable, and unrighteous. But someone remarks, "Then we don't have a free will!" But, oh yes, we do. However, this is precisely the problem. The natural man is free to do what he wants to do and what he wants to do is rebel against God. Isaiah put it aptly: "All we like sheep have gone astray, we have turned every one to his own way" (Isa. 53:6). Thus, we see that our salvation is preceded by an undeniable condition.

In understanding the origin of our salvation, it is also important to note that our salvation is *provided by an unconditional choosing*. Now, if salvation is preceded by an undeniable condition and we can do nothing in and of ourselves to be saved, then God must do something, for we can't. This is exactly what our text says, "I am confident of this very thing, that he who began a good work in you . . . " (Phil. 1:6, NASB). If it is true that in his natural state man is unresponsive, unperceptive, unteachable and unrighteous, then it is certain that the remedy must lie outside of man himself. If indeed man is raised out of spiritual death (that is, born again) and since he is unable to perform the work himself, then we must conclude that God raises us to spiritual life. This is exactly what the text implies: "He which hath begun a good work in you."

God chose you! And this choosing is unconditional. It is not conditioned on your own goodness. The Bible says, "In me (that is, in my flesh,) dwelleth no good thing" (Rom. 7:18). Salvation is provided by an unnconditional choosing.

What doctrine did Jesus preach at the synagogue in Nazareth? "But I tell you of a truth, many widows were in Israel in the days of Elias, when the heaven was shut up three years and six months, when great famine was throughout all the land; But unto none of them was Elias sent, save unto Sarepta, a city of Sidon, unto a woman that was a widow. And many lepers were in Israel in the time of Eliseus the prophet; and none of them were cleansed, saving Naaman the Syrian" (Luke 4:25-27). In the synagogue at Nazareth he preached the fact that salvation was indeed provided by an unconditional choosing. Later he would say in John 15:16, "Ye have not chosen me, but I have chosen you, . . . that ye should go and bring forth fruit." God said to Moses, I will have mercy on whom I will have mercy, and I will have compassion on whom I will have compassion" (Rom. 9:15). Paul began his letter to the Ephesians with these words, "According as he hath chosen us in him before the foundation of the world, that we should be holy and without blame before him in love. Having predestined us unto adoption of children by Jesus Christ to himself, according to the good pleasure of his will" (1:4-5). And in the familiar salvation passage in Ephesians 2, Paul says, "For by grace are ye saved through faith; and that not of yourselves; it is the gift of God: Not of works, lest any man should boast. For we are his workmanship, created in Christ Jesus unto good works *which God hath before ordained that we should walk in them*" (vv. 8-10). And when salvation came to the Gentiles, the Scripture records, "And as many as were ordained to eternal life believed" (Acts 13:48).

God is sovereign. This means he always does what he pleases, and is always pleased with what he does. Our salvation is preceded by an undeniable condition and is provided by an unconditional choosing. This subject of God's choosing is as vast as the universe itself. A few of these key verses from Scripture act as a guide to chart us across this mighty expanse.

The Bible itself is a continuous story of God's unconditional choosing. On the surface many take offense that God chooses us unto salvation. Charles Hadden Spurgeon, the peerless preacher of London in the last century, once exclaimed, "Hardly another church looks upon us favorably." Spurgeon was a mighty defender of the doctrines of grace. It is ironic that many who take offense at the doctrine of God's choosing us unto salvation have no difficulty believing that God chose people in Old Testament times. For instance, they have little difficulty believing God chose Abraham to depart from Ur of the Chaldees, leaving all the rest to heathenism. Also, why should God completely disregard the family laws of Israel and choose young Jacob over his older brother Esau? It is because God is sovereign. You say, "But that is not fair." None of us are deserving of these everlasting mercies of God in being freed of our sin to know him in the free pardon of all our sin. The origin of our salvation is in the heart of God. It is preceded by an undeniable condition and provided by an unconditional choosing.

Third, this salvation is also *procured by an unmistakable calling*. If man is unable to save himself, and if God chooses us unto salvation, then it logically follows that God must provide a means of calling us, procuring salvation for us. It is no secret that our text reads, "He which hath begun a good work in you."

"Whom He predestined, these He also called" (Rom. 8:30, NASB). God not only elects men unto salvation, *he calls them*. I could beg you on my knees, with tears in my eyes, describing the horrors of hell and the glories of heaven, but none of you would come to Christ unless God himself drew you to Jesus.

There are two calls: the outward call and the inward call. Consider the following words of Jesus. "All that the Father giveth me shall come to me; and him that cometh to me I will in no wise cast out" (John 6:37). "No man can come to me, except the Father which hath sent me draw him: and I will raise him up at the last day" (v. 44). "It is written in the prophets, And they shall be all taught of God. Every man therefore that hath heard, and hath learned of the Father, cometh unto me" (v. 45). Do you remember what Jesus said to Simon after the great confession at Caesarea Philippi? "And Jesus answered and said unto him, Blessed art thou Simon Bar-jona; for flesh and blood hath not revealed it unto thee, but my Father which is in heaven" (Matt. 16:17). Paul wrote, "For as many as are led by the Spirit of God, they are the sons of God" (Rom. 8:14). Paul, also writing to the Galatians, said, "But when it pleased God, who separated me from my mother's womb, and called me by his grace . . . " (Gal. 1:15). Peter declared, "But ye are a chosen generation, a royal priesthood, an holy nation, a peculiar people; that you should shew forth the praises of him who hath called you out of darkness into his marvellous light" (1 Pet. 2:9). Later in the same epistle he stated, "But the God of all grace, who hath called us unto his eternal glory by Jesus Christ, after that ye have suffered a while make you perfect, stablish, strengthen, and settle you" (5:10).

How can two people sit on the same pew in the same worship service, sing the same songs, hear the same sermon in the same anointing, and one of these feel absolutely no need of coming to Christ, or anything spiritual in his heart, and the other feel a deep conviction of sin and a longing to know Jesus personally? How can this happen? By the inward call of God.

If you are looking for a Scriptural illustration of this I would point you to Acts 16, the passage concerning the conversion of Lydia. "And a certain woman named Lydia, a seller of purple, from the city of Thyatira, which worshipped God, heard us; *whose heart the Lord opened*, that she attended unto the things that were spoken of Paul" (v. 14). Paul was preaching at the riverside in Philippi. As he preached, he issued the outward call. Then the Lord spoke to Lydia's heart, issuing the inward call. The Holy Spirit chases us down and pursues us, opening our hearts to the gospel.

A few extremists today have carried these doctrines of grace to the point of perverting Scripture by even denying the free offer of the gospel and, in so doing, are setting their camps dangerously close to the border of heresy. But the fact that salvation is God's work and he takes the initiative in calling us does not diminish one's intensity in preaching the gospel to every creature and sharing the outward call with every last person on this planet! We have a Great Commission to "preach the gospel to every creature" (Mark 16:15). This is why these doctrines of grace should intensify our evangelistic efforts. We are to proclaim to the world the outward call and then trust in the Holy Spirit to issue the inward call. This also is what happened at the grave of Lazarus. There was the outward call, a response for the people, that is: roll away the stone, then loose him, and let him go. The truth of the matter is, only Jesus could give life, and it was the inward call to Lazarus's heart from the words of Jesus that brought about life and quickened his dead body.

Now, what about the origin of our salvation? The truth is: it is not so much "I decided to follow Jesus," "I repented," or "I came to Christ." The fact is, "He which hath begun a good work in you." The Scripture says, "You hath he quickened who were dead in trespasses and sins" (Eph. 2:1). Our salvation is preceded by an undeniable condition, provided by an unconditional choosing, and procured by an unmistakable calling. This was the theology and message which thundered forth from the pulpits and pews of such men as Bunyan, Spurgeon, Carey, Whitefield, Edwards, and our own Southern Baptist forefathers, James P. Boyce and John A. Broadus, founders of The Southern Baptist Theological Seminary, and B. H. Carroll, founder of Southwestern Baptist Theological Seminary.

Many are confused on the issue of "whosoever will may come." But this brings all the whosoevers into the focus of real spiritual light. Yes, whosoever will may come! Send the proclamation far and wide. Believe it! Preach it! For no one will truly come who has not first been drawn by the Father to the Lord Jesus (see John 6:44).

Thus, the origin of our salvation is God himself. It is God who does the redeeming. The Bible says, "Forasmuch as ye know that ye were not redeemed with corruptible things, as silver and gold, from your vain conversation received by tradition from your fathers; But with the precious blood of Christ, as of a lamb without blemish and without spot" (1 Pet. 1:18-19). God wants to begin the good work in many today. As you hear the gospel preached, or even as you read a book such as this, you hear the outward call. Now, the Holy Spirit issues the inward call to your heart. As he did Lydia, he may be opening your heart right now, convicting you of your sin, and convincing you of his righteousness. You can't do it on your own. The truth is most of us have tried a thousand times—but God can right now! Our part is to believe and receive. "But as many as received Him, to them gave he power to become the sons of God" (John 1:12). "If thou shalt confess with thy mouth the Lord Jesus, and shalt believe in thine heart that God hath raised him from the dead, thou shalt be saved" (Rom. 10:9).

This text not only deals with the origin of our salvation but also goes on to examine:

The Outcome of Our Salvation

He who began a good work in you will perfect it until the day of Christ Jesus (Phil. 1:6*b*, NASB).

What is the outcome of this marvelous salvation provided by God? What does it mean to us personally? It means we are secure. We are secure in the "now" life and secure in the "next" life.

Note initially in the outcome of our salvation that we are *secure in the now life.* Our text says that God will "perfect it until the day of Christ Jesus." What good news! We are secure in the now life. God will perform our salvation not just in heaven but *until* the day of Christ Jesus. We are living today in the "great until." An unknown poet has written:

> We watch for our Savior and Bridegroom
> who loves us and made us His own.
> For Him we are looking and longing,
> for Jesus and Jesus alone.

But until then, he will perfect that which concerns us. He who began this good work in us is the same one who will perform it. We are neither saved by good works nor kept by good works. "He who began a good work in you will perfect it until the day of Christ Jesus." I am always a little amused by people who are quick to testify they are saved by faith and yet continue to live their lives by reason, not by faith. If faith is good enough to save us, faith is also good enough to live by.

If man takes the initiative in salvation, he must retain responsibility for the final outcome. But the Bible says, "He which hath begun a good work in you will perform it until the day of Christ Jesus." We are kept by the Lord Jesus Christ.

It is extremely important to know we are secure in the now life. I recall upon our family's moving to Fort Lauderdale an unforgettable experience which continually happened in those early weeks. The hustle and bustle of a metropolitan area of over a million people was a long distance from the quiet little Oklahoma town we had called home only a few weeks earlier. Our oldest daughter, Wendy, was four years old at the time. I remember vividly how each time we would leave our new home and drive in the strange surroundings, with endless lines of traffic, how she was obsessed with a question with which I would be continually bombarded—"We will be able to get home, won't we, Daddy?" That's very important for a child, to know that she will be able to get home. And it is also very important for a child of God. How important to know we are going to be able to get home, that we do not have to wonder from day to day if we are saved or lost, but that he "will perfect the good work in us until the day of Christ Jesus." Yes, indeed, we are secure in the now life.

We live in such an uncertain world. A world that is uncertain politically, economically, materially, socially, nationally, internationally, and uncertain on every hand. But amid all this uncertainty, God tells us we can be secure in the now life. The Bible says, "These things I have written to you who believe in the name of the Son of God, in order that you may *know* that you have eternal life" (1 John 5:13, NASB, author's italics).

The Word of God was given that we may know we can be secure in the now life. How can we know? The Bible says, "these things are written." We do not know we have eternal life by our feelings. Some mornings upon rising I don't feel very well. If my salvation were determined by my feelings I would be saved and lost from day to day. The Bible says we can know that we are saved because "these things are written." What things?

How about, "Him that cometh to me I will in no wise cast out" (John 6:37)? How about John 5:24, "Verily, verily I say unto you He that heareth my word, and believeth on him that sent me, hath everlasting life, and shall not come under condemnation; but is passed from death unto life"? How about John 10:27-28, "My sheep hear My voice, and I know them, and they follow Me; and I give eternal life to them, and they shall never perish; and no one shall snatch them out of my hand" (NASB)? Yes, "These things have I written to you who believe in the Son of God, in order that you may know that you have eternal life" (1 John 5:13, NASB). Our eternal security is not a matter of our "holding on" until the end. The truth is, God is holding us and "no man can pluck us out of his hand" (John 10:29).

The Bible does not say, "These things have I written unto you who believe on the name of the Son of God that you may *hope* that you have eternal life." Nor does it say, "These things have I written unto you who believe on the name of the Son of God that you may *wish* that you have eternal life." Nor does it say, "These things have I written unto you who believe on the name of the Son of God that you may *think* that you have eternal life." The Bible says, "These things have I written unto you who believe on the name of the Son of God that you may know that you have eternal life" (NASB). What is the outcome of our salvation? It is secure in the now life!

I remember when our little daughter began to walk. She would reach up with her chubby little fingers, grab my index finger, and hang on with all of her might. She would take a step or two, let go, and fall to the ground. It didn't take too long before Daddy learned an important lesson. I would reach down, grab hold of her hand, and then when she stumbled, Dad would be there to hold her up and teach her to walk. What a perfect analogy of our Heavenly Father and us. Our salvation is not a matter of our holding on to the bitter

end. He reaches down and grabs hold of us, and when we
stumble he is always there to help his dear children along.
This is why we sing:

> Blessed assurance, Jesus is mine!
> Oh, what a foretaste of glory divine!
> Heir of salvation, purchase of God,
> Born of his Spirit, wash'd in his blood.
>
> FANNY J. CROSBY

We can have this blessed assurance because our salvation is
secure in the now life.

In examining the outcome of our salvation, it is vital to
know our salvation is not only secure in the now life but also
in the next life. Paul says, "He who began a good work in you
will perfect it until the day of Christ Jesus." Jesus said, "This is
the will of Him who sent Me, that of all that He has given Me,
I lose nothing, but raise it up on the last day" (John 6:39,
NASB). Yes, we are secure in the next life as well as the now
life. Paul wrote to the Thessalonians:

> But I would not have you to be ignorant, brethren, concerning
> them which are asleep, that ye sorrow not, even as others which
> have no hope. For if we believe that Jesus died and rose again,
> even so them also which sleep in Jesus will God bring with him.
> For this we say unto you by the word of the Lord, that we which
> are alive and remain unto the coming of the Lord shall not
> prevent them which are asleep. For the Lord himself shall
> descend from heaven with a shout, with the voice of the
> archangel, and with the trump of God: and the dead in Christ
> shall rise first: Then we which are alive and remain shall be
> caught up together with them in the clouds, to meet the Lord in
> the air: and so shall we ever be with the Lord. Wherefore
> comfort one another with these words" (1 Thess. 4:13-18).

One of the surest realities is that Jesus Christ is personally
returning to planet Earth. The dead in Christ are going to
rise, and then we who are alive and remain will be caught up
together with them in the clouds (raptured) to meet the Lord

in the air! What a day—glorious day—that will be!

We are secure in the next life as the bride of Christ. The day of Christ Jesus will feature a marvelous wedding referred to in Scripture as the "marriage of the Lamb." Jewish weddings in biblical times throw considerable light on this feast. First, there was the stage of the marriage covenant. Here the groom would leave his father's house and travel to the home of his prospective bride to settle and pay a purchase price. The second stage would come when, once the agreement was made, the bride and groom would drink wine as a symbol of unity. Now, they were considered married, although they did not begin living together. The groom had to prepare a place for his bride. The third stage came at the end of that time. When the groom had prepared the place, he would come at an unannounced time. When people in the neighborhood saw him coming, they would begin to shout, "Behold the bridegroom cometh," thus forewarning the bride to get ready. The fourth stage would entail the groom's getting the bride and taking her to his father's house for the wedding ceremony. Now, "He who began a good work in [us] will perfect it until the day of Christ Jesus." We are secure in the now life and the next life.

Just as the Jewish bridegroom left his father's house, traveling to the home of his prospective bride to pay the purchase price, so the Lord Jesus Christ, two thousand years ago, left the glories of heaven and his Father's house to enter this sin-cursed earth to pay the price for our salvation. He purchased us with his own blood on Calvary. "For ye are bought with a price: therefore glorify God in your body, and in your spirit, which are God's" (1 Cor. 6:20).

Then, as the agreement was made, and the Jewish bride and groom drank wine as the symbol of unity, so the Lord Jesus Christ the evening before the crucifixion took the cup as a symbol of our unity with him. Just as the Jewish bridegroom then returned to his father's house to prepare a place for his

bride, so the Lord Jesus Christ, before Calvary, declared, "I go
to prepare a place for you. If I go and prepare a place for you,
I will come again, and receive you unto myself; that where I
am, there ye may be also" (John 14:2-3). Next, just as the
Jewish bridegroom, at an unannounced time after the prepa-
ration had been made, came to receive his bride, so the Lord
Jesus at an unannounced time and with a loud shout will
come to receive his bride, those of us who are redeemed.
And, just as people would begin to shout, "Behold the
bridegroom cometh," there are many pulpits across the world
that are making the shout loud and clear today. As Bible
prophecies are fulfilled and events point to the coming of
Christ, many preachers are beginning to shout at the top of
their lungs, "Behold, the bridegroom cometh." And finally,
just as the Jewish bridegroom would receive his new bride
and take her away to the father's house for the wedding
ceremony, so the Lord Jesus Christ will come and receive us,
taking us away to the great marriage supper of the Lamb. "He
who began a good work in [us] will perfect it until the day of
Christ Jesus."

When a bride is about to be married, I have noticed that she
takes two important courses of action. One, she accepts the
invitation of the bridegroom. Obviously, without this acceptance there would be no wedding. Two, she makes herself as
lovely as she can for the ceremony.

The question is, have we accepted the invitation of our
bridegroom, the Lord Jesus? If so, are we making ourselves as
lovely as we can for the wedding? "He who began a good
work in [us] will perfect it until the day of Christ Jesus."

We are living in the "great until." Until . . . the day of Christ
Jesus! We can trust the Lord and know we are secure in this
life and the next.

The apostle Paul said, "For I am confident of this very thing,
that He who began a good work in you will perfect it until the
day of Christ Jesus" (Phil. 1:6, NASB). Without this confi-

dence, Paul never could have withstood the stoning at Lystra, the shipwreck at Malta, imprisonment at Rome, or his martyr's death. Oh, that we can be confident in Christ! Do you have this confidence? It only comes in knowing Jesus Christ.

The origin of our salvation is in God himself. "He hath begun the good work in us." To recap, it is first preceded by an undeniable condition. The natural man is unresponsive, unperceptive, unteachable, and unrighteous. Two, our salvation is provided by an unconditional choosing. Since our undeniable condition is that we will not come to Christ, then God must do something, for we can't. He is the one who began the good work in us. Three, our salvation is procured by an unmistakable calling. If indeed we are unable to save ourselves, and if God chooses us unto salvation, then it logically follows that God provides a means of calling, procuring salvation for us. "He hath begun a good work in us."

And what an outcome our salvation promises! We are secure in the "now" life and secure in the "next" life. Yes, "He which hath begun a good work in [us] *will* perform it until the day of Jesus Christ." We are confident of this very thing! And this confidence is essential in understanding our salvation.

5.
The Forgotten Word in Positive Preaching

Now in those days John the Baptist came, preaching in the wilderness of Judea, saying, "Repent, for the kingdom of heaven is at hand" (Matt. 3:1-2).

There is a new phenomenon sweeping Christendom today. It is the rapid rise of the high-profile preachers with their messages of prosperity and positive thinking. Now, is there a planned program of prosperity in the Scripture? There is certainly no premium on poverty. Luke 6:38 says, "Give, and it shall be given unto you; good measure, pressed down, and shaken together and running over, shall men give into your bosom. For with the same measure that ye mete withal it shall be measured to you again."

Also, I strongly adhere to the fact that followers of Jesus should be positive thinkers. The Scripture affirms that "we can do all things through Christ who strengthens us." Yet, the gospel being preached in many places today is not a complete gospel. There is currently a forgotten word in positive preaching.

The word? *Repentance!* When was the last time you turned on your television set to hear a preacher of the gospel thundering forth the message of repentance? When was the last time you read a book on the need of repentance? Pulpits and preachers are strangely silent today regarding the message of repentance.

This was the heart cry not only of John the Baptist who thundered forth, "Repent, for the kingdom of heaven is at hand," but of Jesus himself who repeatedly called people to "repent and believe the gospel." Strange, isn't it, how silent many of our pulpits have been? There are many preachers today who are soothingly, softly whispering "believe, believe, believe." This positive preaching is popular because it calls for no change of life-style. While many whisper "believe," too few are proclaiming the message of the Bible, "Repent." Repentance is the forgotten word in positive preaching.

John the Baptist, the forerunner of our Lord, came preaching in the wilderness of Judea, saying, "Repent, for the kingdom of heaven is at hand." Many do not preach this message because they are uncertain about what is involved in repentance. I fear that it is not only the forgotten word in positive preaching but also one of the most perverted words in our Christian vocabulary. What does it really mean to repent? What actually is the call to repentance? In the words of Matthew 3:2 it is evident that a personal mandate commands repentance, and a positive motive commends repentance. Let's begin by noting that:

A Personal Mandate Commands It

Repent ye (Matt. 3:2a).

Here is a personal mandate to each of us. "Repent ye! . . . You repent." The mandate is that we should repent. Before one can genuinely repent one must know what it is to repent. Consequently, as we examine this personal mandate we are going to ask three very pertinent questions. What is it? Why is it important? Where is it?

First, what is repentance? There is considerable confusion regarding the question, "What is it?" Let's note what it is not. Repentance is not *remorse*. That is, it's not simply being sorry for one's sin. Remorse may lead to repentance, but remorse is not repentance. If you recall, the rich young ruler went away sorrowful when Jesus told him the cost of following. He was remorseful but did not repent. Too many have substituted remorse for repentance, and this is the reason they flounder in the faith.

Note also that repentance is not *regret*. That is, merely wishing that the deed had not happened. There are many people who regret their sin yet have never repented. Pontius Pilate, who betrayed our Lord, took the basin of water and washed his hands, regretting his evil deed, wishing it hadn't happened. But he did not repent. Many substitute regret for repentance and tragically fool themselves in the process.

Also, we should note that repentance is not just *resolve*. All of us have made New Year's resolutions. Many of us have resolved to assume a new set of moral standards and life on higher plains, but it never seems really to "take" with most of us because we substitute resolve for repentance. Repentance is not remorse, regret, or resolve.

Finally, repentance is not *reform*. That is, turning over a new leaf. Perhaps this reformation even involves restitution. It was so in the case of Judas Iscariot. After having betrayed our Lord he took the thirty pieces of silver back to the Temple area and threw it at those who had paid the price of betrayal. Judas reformed but, unfortunately, did not repent. There are many people who have substituted reform for repentance. John the Baptist did not say, "Reform, for the kingdom of heaven is at hand." Nor did he say, "Make resolutions, for the kingdom of heaven is at hand." Nor did he say, "Regret your deeds, for the kingdom of heaven is at hand." Nor did he say, "Have remorse, for the kingdom of heaven is at hand." He declared the message of the Bible, "Repent: for the kingdom of heaven is at hand!"

Having seen what repentance is not, let's examine what it actually is. Is repentance turning from every sin as some people teach today? If so, who has repented? In the upcoming pages I will unfold these answers. When you came to Christ, did you turn from every sin? The truth is, in our natural state we are dead, not sick but dead, and unresponsive to the gospel of Christ. "But the natural man receiveth not the things of the Spirit of God: for they are foolishness unto him: neither can he know them, because they are spiritually discerned" (1 Cor. 2:14). The word *repent (metanoeō)* in its original language is defined as "a change of mind." This is to change one's way of thinking about salvation. "There is a way which seemeth right unto a man, but the end thereof are the ways of death," (Prov. 14:12). Repentance takes place when a man or a woman changes his or her mind about the things of God.

Repentance makes one love what one once hated and hate what one once loved. When I was converted at the age of seventeen, I had never heard of the word *repentance*. In fact, it was some weeks, or perhaps months, after my conversion before I ever heard the word. But I know that I repented! How do I know? The things I used to love to do I no longer desired, and the things I never thought I would like to do became the things that I loved to do. It was a change of mind. Repentance makes one love what one once hated and hate what one once loved.

Repentance is a change of mind! This change of mind is always evidenced in three ways. First, the *attitude*—that is, intellectually. As stated, it is a change of mind. Here is where we begin. This is repentance. Second, the *affections*—there is a change emotionally. This is a change of heart. Now if we have genuinely had a change of mind, then a change of heart will follow. Third, the *actions*. In other words, there comes a change in our volition. This is a change of the will. The truth is if I have genuinely changed my mind, my heart will have been changed, and if my heart has been changed, then a change in volition is certain to follow.

Repentance is a change of mind. A person may be moved to tears emotionally by a sermon. This may fill one's heart with remorse or regret, but it is not necessarily repentance. A person may have his will manipulated by various means, but if he has not repented (changed his mind) he is not saved.

Didn't Jesus say, "Except ye repent, ye shall all likewise perish" (Luke 13:3)?

We find our most obvious biblical illustration of repentance in Luke 15 with the well-known story of the prodigal son. Here was a young man who had gone out into the far country and wasted all of his substance in riotous, ungodly living. He was far away from his father's house. First of all, this boy came to have a change of *attitude*. Luke 15:17*a* says, "He came to himself." He changed his mind. Then what happened? He had a change of *affections*. He said, "How many hired servants of my father's have bread enough and to spare, and I perish with hunger. I will arise and go to my father, and say . . . I have sinned against heaven, and before thee, And am no more worthy to be called thy son" (vv. 17*b*-18). His heart changed. Then what happened when he had a change of mind and a change of heart? He had a change of *action*. His will changed. He said, "I *will* arise and go to my father." And verse 20 states, "He arose."

The prodigal son had a change of mind (repentance) and it was evident in four areas. First, he regretted the deed. He came to himself and said, "How many hired servants of my father's have bread enough and to spare, and I perish with hunger." When his mind was changed, he regretted his deed. Second, note that he blamed himself for his sin. He said, "I will arise and go to my father, and say . . . I have sinned against heaven, and before thee." He took the responsibility. He blamed himself for his sin. Third, he acknowledged the Father's right to be displeased. He said to his father, "[I] am no more worthy to be called thy son." And finally, he resolved to sin no more. The Bible says, "He arose, and came to his father." Repentance is a change of mind. The battle is in the mind, and the proof is in these four areas. Each of us will repent when we change our minds. And in changing our minds surely our hearts will be changed and our wills will

follow. This change of mind will cause us to regret our deed,
to blame ourselves for it, to acknowledge God's right to be
displeased with us, and to resolve to set our face toward
Jesus.

What is repentance? It is a change of mind. It is plain to see
that no one can be saved without repentance.

Let's now examine our second question. Why is it important? In other words, why is repentance so important? Jesus
said, "Except ye repent; ye shall all likewise perish." Why is it
important? To begin with, it was the message of the Old
Testament prophets. All of them were preachers of repentance. As far back as Noah we hear them calling on the people
to forsake their wicked ways and turn to the Lord.

What was the message of John the Baptist? Matthew 3:2
says, "Repent, for the kingdom of heaven is at hand." And
Matthew 3:7-8 says, "But when he saw many of the Pharisees
and Sadducees coming for baptism, he said to them, 'You
brood of vipers, who warned you to flee from the wrath to
come?' Therefore bring forth fruit in keeping with repentance" (NASB).

What was the message of our Lord Jesus himself? Jesus
commenced his ministry with the message of repentance.
"From that time Jesus began to preach, and to say, 'Repent:
for the kingdom of heaven is at hand'" (Matt. 4:17). And in
Mark 1:14-15 we read, "And after John had been taken into
custody, Jesus came into Galilee, preaching the gospel of
God, and saying, 'The time is fulfilled, and the kingdom of
God is at hand; repent and believe in the gospel'" (NASB).
Jesus *continued* his ministry with the message of repentance.
"I tell you, no, but unless you repent you will all likewise
perish" (Luke 13:3, NASB). The burden of his heart was in a
word, *repent*. But not only did Jesus commence and continue
his ministry, he *concluded* his ministry with the word *repentance*. In Luke 24:46-47 our Lord says, "Thus it is written, that
the Christ should suffer and rise again from the dead the

third day; and that repentance for forgiveness of sins should be proclaimed in His name to all the nations, beginning from Jerusalem" (NASB).

Here is the message of the Great Commission. In Matthew's account of the Great Commission, God gives us the *mechanics*. We are to "make" disciples, "mark" them by baptism, and "mature" them in the faith. These are the mechanics of the Great Commission. In Mark's account of the Great Commission he gives us the *measure* of it. We are to take this gospel to the whole world. And in Luke's account of the Great Commission he gives us the *message* of this commission. And what is it? "That repentance and remission of sins should be preached in . . . all nations" (24:47). Thus Jesus commenced, continued, and concluded his ministry with the same word—*"Repent."* How can a minister claim to be preaching the gospel if he leaves out the heart of Jesus' own message?

What about the message of the apostles? "And they went out, and preached that men should repent" (Mark 6:12). They went out and preached. What did they preach? Prosperity? Faith only? They preached that people should repent!

What was the message of Simon Peter? Hear him preach at Pentecost and after that mighty sermon hear them ask, "What shall we do?" Quickly came the reply, "Repent" (Acts 2:37-38).

What was the message of Paul? Acts 17:30 says "Therefore having overlooked the times of ignorance, God is now declaring to men that all everywhere should repent" (NASB). And Acts 20:21 states, "Solemnly testifying to both Jews and Greeks of repentance toward God and faith in our Lord Jesus Christ" (NASB).

What was the message of John the Beloved? All one need do is turn to the messages to the churches of Asia recorded in the Book of Revelation and find that eight times in the letters to the seven churches he peals forth the message of repentance. Why is it important? Because it is the message of the Bible.

What was the message of the Bible? What was the message of the early church? Was it positive thinking with all sorts of trinkets for reminders? Was it concentrated ministries on the home, finance, or other selected "professional ministries?" Was it the constant theme of the second coming of our Lord Jesus Christ? No! In a word, the message of the early church was, "Repent!" You see, if a man repented they knew he would be a positive thinker, he would become the head of his home—all these other matters would fall into place. Do you know why we have all these specialized "professional ministries" in the United States today? Because men have need of repentance. We read nothing in the New Testament about these types of ministries. Their ministry was the word, *repent*. When a man genuinely repented, he got his home in order. We can preach to people about the home and the chain of authority, prosperity, and positive thinking until we are blue in the face, but Jesus said, "Except ye repent, ye shall all likewise perish."

It is strange how silent many preachers are today concerning repentance. I am convinced it is because many preachers have lost sight of the sinfulness of man. Some are preaching who deny the Bible truth of a literal, burning hell or at least seldom, if ever, mention it. There are many who are preaching today who hold to doctrines of universalism, believing that everyone will be saved. Consequently, what need is there of the message of repentance? Too many churches and preachers have lost sight of the lostness of man and the holiness of God.

Perhaps this is because repentance is not a very popular message. It cost John the Baptist his head. It helped crucify our Lord Jesus. It is indeed far more popular to tickle the ears of our listeners with messages of "comfort" and "sweetness and light."

Why is repentance important? Because it is the message of the Bible. With so much emphasis in the New Testament upon repentance it is strange how few voices preach it today.

Let's note our third question as we see that this personal mandate commands repentance. *Where is it?* That is, where is repentance in salvation? Does repentance precede faith? Or, does faith precede repentance? Think about it: Does one repent before one can exercise faith? Or, does one exercise faith before one repents? If you believe repentance is turning from every sin, then faith must come first, for repentance would then become a works salvation. This is the idea of many today. But, if repentance is turning from every sin, then who has repented? Who of us has turned from every sin?

Conversely, if you believe that repentance is indeed a change of mind, then repentance is first in the order, for one must change one's way of thinking before one can grasp the free promise of the grace of God in Christ Jesus. Now, since mankind is totally depraved and since God sovereignly calls us unto himself, it stands to reason that God then must grant repentance to us for we cannot obtain it in our depraved condition. This is exactly what the Bible teaches. Take for example 2 Timothy 2:24-25, "And the Lord's bond-servant must not be quarrelsome, but be kind to all, able to teach, patient when wronged, with gentleness correcting those who are in opposition, if perhaps *God may grant them repentance* leading to the knowledge of the truth" (NASB, author's italics). Repentance is the gift of God's grace that transforms the mind. And when the attitude is genuinely transformed, the affections are changed. And, when the affections are changed, the action (will) is changed.

Faith and repentance are as much the gifts of God as the Savior upon whom our faith rests. Salvation is, from first to last, all of grace. Note Acts 5:31, "He is the one whom God exalted to His right hand as a Prince and a Savior, *to grant repentance* to Israel, and forgiveness of sins" (NASB, author's italics). The truth is, our Lord Jesus has gone up that grace may come down. Repentance is the gift of God; it is granted by God's grace. Acts 11:18 says, "And when they heard this, they quieted down, and glorified God, saying, "Well, then, *God has granted to the Gentiles also the repentance* that leads to life" (NASB, author's italics).

The truth of Scripture is that repentance and faith are different sides of the same coin. Charles Haddon Spurgeon said it well: "Repentance and faith are born at the same time; they are Siamese twins." We cannot have faith without repentance and we cannot repent without faith. D. James Kennedy says, "Repentance itself will not save you, yet you cannot be saved without it."

Repentance and faith are inseparable in Scripture. Time and time again the words are linked together, "Repent and believe." Now, you may have a false faith (intellectual assent) which brings no change of life-style. Many people are walking this way today. They have adhered to only half of the gospel message, and consequently they have nothing more than an intellectual assent to the claims of Christ. If your faith doesn't cause you to live life on a higher plain, it is a false faith. Or you may have a false repentance with no faith which simply causes you to rely upon your own efforts or works. What frustration and drudgery this brings to many lives!

Repentance and faith are inseparable. There has never been anyone who repented of their sin who was not forgiven, and there has never been anyone who has been forgiven who has not repented! It will help us to remember at this point that it is not repentance which forgives us. It is the blood of our Lord Jesus Christ which "cleanses us from all sin." Repentance and faith are the gift of God and they are inseparable.

Now, do you see what happens? God calls a person to the Lord Jesus. By his grace he pulls at the heart strings of that person and leads him to Jesus Christ. The person comes to Christ, saying, "I give to Jesus my all. Just as I am I come." The regeneration process takes place as the Holy Spirit does his work. This produces repentance and faith (the gifts of

God's grace). Salvation is by grace through faith. The person repents (changes his mind about the way of salvation). How do we know? The Holy Spirit changes one's heart. How do we know? One's mind is changed. One's heart is changed. Then the Holy Spirit begins to change one's will and one says with the prodigal son, "I *will* arise and come to Jesus."

So repentance is perhaps best defined in the words of Dr. R. T. Kendall (of the world-famed Westminster Chapel in London) as "agreeing with God." This indeed is New Testament repentance. "If we confess our sins, he is faithful and just to forgive us our sins, and to cleanse us from all unrighteousness" (1 John 1:9). Confession is an essential sign of genuine repentance (a change of mind). Thus, the call of the hour is to join the prophets of old, John the Baptist, Peter, Paul, John the Beloved, and our Lord with the message, "Repent ye: for the kingdom of heaven is at hand." A personal mandate commands it. "Repent." Change your mind! There is indeed "a way which seemeth right unto a man, but the end thereof are the ways of death." Change your mind—a personal mandate commands it.

Note second that not only a personal mandate commands it but:

A Positive Motive Commends It

For the kingdom of heaven is at hand (Matt. 3:2*b*).

There is a popular slogan we often hear repeated and see on bumper stickers across America. The simple message says, *turn or burn*. This is the idea of many! But while it is true that unless we turn to Jesus we will spend eternity in a Godless, eternal, burning hell, it is also true that the fear of punishment is not the primary motive for repentance. There is a positive motive which commends it. John said, "Repent ye." Why? *for the kingdom of heaven is at hand*. The emphasis is not to repent for fear of punishment but because of the goodness of God's grace! If you are in need of repentance today, "Repent ye: for the kingdom of heaven is at hand."

Listen to Romans 2:4: "Or do you think lightly of the riches
of His kindness and forbearance and patience, not knowing
that the kindness of God leads you to repentance?" (NASB).
The King James Version says "goodness" instead of "kindness." We are so privileged to hear the gospel today. We are so
privileged to read these words. Not because they are written
by my pen but because they contain the message of the
gospel; the gospel which millions of people on our planet
have never heard. The missionary's feet have never walked in
their little villages. A copy of God's Word has never been
translated into their language or dialect and thus they die in
darkness. Millions are going downward. And you? You are
placed in the very focus of the Christian life, and yet you have
no time for Jesus. Can't you understand that it is the
goodness of God which is allowing you to hear the gospel,
and that this is what leads you to repentance today? "Repent
ye: for the kingdom of heaven is at hand."

Note that Romans 2:4 does not say that "the kindness of
God *calls* you to repentance." But it says, "the kindness of God
leads you to repentance." The truth is God calls us to repentance by the gospel. But God leads us to repentance by his
goodness. The goodness of God comes to us where we are,
takes us by the hand, as though we were a little child, and
leads us to repentance. It is the goodness of God that leads us
to repentance. A positive motive commands it.

My family and I vacation each summer in a quaint, little
village nestled in the Great Smoky Mountains. It is a refresh-
ing retreat from the massive traffic jams and the hustle and
bustle of Fort Lauderdale. In fact, it is like stepping into a time
tunnel. There are sights and sounds we do not see and hear in
our metropolis. The idea of a traffic jam in our little mountain
hamlet is two cars getting to an intersection at the same time.
The women there still hang their clothes out on lines in the
backyard, people still use those little, wood-burning pot-

bellied stoves, there are gravel roads and cattle gaps and white picket fences, the cafe down in the valley serves fresh home-grown and home-cooked vegetables, and they still have telephone party lines. It is incredible!

On a recent trip there our family spent a week in an old, white farm house on the side of the mountain. It was a beautiful spot but a little "scary" for our two little "city girls." The children slept upstairs and the whole house creaked when anyone took a step. That first night happened to be one of those pitch dark summer nights in the Smokies. As James Weldon Johnson put it in *God's Trombones*, it was "blacker than a hundred midnights down in a cypress swamp." I was awakened in the middle of the night by the cries upstairs of our seven-year-old daughter. I bounded up the stairs to find her standing in the dark, calling for Mom and Dad. Taking her by the hand, I led her down the steps into the security of our own bed where she soundly slept the rest of the night away.

And so our dear Heavenly Father finds us in the dark, takes us by the hand, and as the Bible says, "leads us to repentance."

Repent ye . . . for the kingdom of heaven is at hand. The kingdom of heaven is the rule of Christ, not only tomorrow in the coming kingdom, but today—right now. It is the rule of Christ not merely in the kingdom of glory, which is to come when the lion will lie down with the lamb (and the lamb will not be in the lion's stomach), and there will be a thousand years of perfect peace upon the earth. But it is the kingdom of grace—right here and right now. It is the reign of Christ in our lives now. Repent ye, for the kingdom of heaven is at hand. The Lord Jesus want to rule and reign in your life *now* as you submit to his lordship.

The truth is, the more we try to "work up repentance" the more we fail, but if we would think of our Lord Jesus Christ shedding his precious blood for us on Calvary's cross, God

taking us by the hand with his goodness in leading us to
Jesus, repentance would burst forth. If you can say, "O, Jesus
washed all my sins away" flippantly; if you can sing, "All my
sins are gone, all because of Calvary," and sing it with no real
meaning in your heart; if you never shed a tear over Calvary;
or never sense a deep indebtedness to our Lord Jesus, then
you do not know the meaning of repentance.

On the other hand, many have repented. Their lives have
been gloriously transformed through a change of their minds.
And all this time they have not known what to call it. This is
beautiful to behold in the changed lives of many.

Repent ye . . . for the kingdom of heaven is at hand. A
positive motive commends it. Tell someone only to repent
and you leave them wounded by the wayside. Tell someone to
repent *for the kingdom of heaven is at hand*, with all of its light,
healing, glory, and redemption, and you preach a complete
gospel to him. The change associated with the word *repentance* must be followed with the challenge of the words, *the
kingdom of heaven is at hand*. Some preach only the negative
portion of the gospel and leave people guilty and depressed.
But a positive motive commends it, "Repent ye: for the
kingdom of heaven is at hand."

It is time that we take seriously the message of repentance.
Perhaps many of us reading these words need to join the
prodigal son in "coming to ourselves." That is, we need to
change our minds about the way of life. And once our minds
have genuinely been changed, our hearts will be changed.
Frustration comes in many lives because folks are trying to
seek a change of heart who've never changed their minds.
They never have taken personal responsibility for sin. The
truth is, once our minds and hearts have changed, our
volitions will follow. The reason many people can never will
to do what is right is: they never come to a change of mind.
What difference does it make if we drive the most luxurious
cars that money can buy. What difference does it make if we

eat vitamin-enriched foods? What difference does it make if we wear thousand-dollar suits? What difference does it make if we sleep on a name-brand mattress? What difference does it make if we live in a mansion by the ocean? What difference does it make if we are placed in a ten-thousand-dollar mahogany casket and buried in a cemetery that is as lovely as a botanical garden, and rise up in judgment to face a God we do not know? *Except a man repent . . . he shall perish.*

"Repent ye: for the kingdom of heaven is at hand." A personal mandate commands it. "Repent ye." What is it? A change of mind. Why is it? It is important because it is the message of the entire Bible. Where is it? Repentance and faith are inseparable gifts of God's grace, granted by the Father himself. But, that's not all. A positive motive commends it.

"Repent ye" . . . for the kingdom of heaven, with all of its light, glory, and grace is at hand!

6.
Praying for the Sick

Is anyone among you sick? Let him call for the elders of the church, and let them pray over him, anointing him with oil in the name of the Lord; and the prayer offered in faith will restore the one who is sick, and the Lord will raise him up, and if he has committed sins, they will be forgiven him (Jas. 5:14-15, NASB).

There is much confusion today regarding the area of intercession, and particularly intercession for those who are sick. If there ever was an area where modern-day angels fear to tread, here it is! So much extremism on one hand has led the mainstream of evangelicals to maintain a hands-off policy in praying for the sick. This is unfortunate in that it is one of the most particular and specific ministries given to the local church. Since devoting a time every week to praying for the sick, our local expression of the body of Christ here in Fort Lauderdale has discovered a new power and authority in advancing the kingdom of God in our "Jerusalem."

The churches of my denomination are well known for our mid-week prayer meetings. Our churches around the world meet every Wednesday evening to pray and remember those who are hospitalized, shut-in, or sick. We believe in divine healing. The only problem most of us have is when someone is healed! To be quite honest, I used to pass over these verses in James with little comment. Many of us are so programmed against the supernatural that we are afraid to ask miracle's from God. We somehow have the erroneous idea that our God-given call is to protect God's reputation. After all, if we should pray the prayer of faith for the sick we might make God look bad. Isn't that unbelievable? And yet, many readers are fearful of these very verses for the same reason. I am becoming convinced that when we meet together as a family of God, if something doesn't happen that is supernatural, then it is superficial.

I believe man is made up of three parts—spirit, soul, and body. We are vocal, intense, and quick to talk about the needs of the spirit. Although we waver a little, we are also vocal in speaking of the needs in the soulish realm, our emotions and hurts. Why are we so silent today regarding the needs of the physical? In praying for others, why do we only pray for two thirds of their being? We pray for their spirits. We want them to be saved and grow in the Lord. We pray for their souls. We want them to be healed of hurt feelings and to be emotionally stable, but the church is strangely silent today in praying for the needs of the body.

There is a tremendous paradox here. While God's directive in James 5:14-15 is clear, the church tends to ignore it. In these verses the Bible offers a solution to one of mankind's greatest problems and needs. And in the midst of this solution, the church by and large ignores it. These instructions in praying for the sick are as specific and directive as the ones given to Paul in 1 Corinthians 11 for administering the Lord's Supper. A new day of power would dawn on the church of the Lord Jesus if we would take as serious the directives in praying for the sick.

There is an open door for churches who will dare to be different and become known as houses of prayer. If people have spiritual needs, they need to know there is a church which will pray for their needs. If people have emotional, soulish needs, they need to realize there is a church which will pray for their inner healing. If people have physical needs, they too need to be aware that there is a church which will pray for their healing.

What does the Bible have to say about praying for the sick? In James 5 we will examine the probe, the proposal, the procedure, the prayer, and the provision in praying for the

sick, trusting that many will be moved to a ministry of prayer.
First, note:

The Probe

Is there any sick among you? (Jas. 5:14)

In praying for the sick we begin with the probe. God asks
the question, "Is there any sick among you?" This brings us to
an initial and vital question—why are people sick? While
there are many answers to this question, we will deal here
with a few of the most apparent biblical ones. Some are sick
because they *break natural laws*. Some people burn the candle
at both ends, rest little, and simply burn themselves out.
Some people have cancer of the lungs and are sick because
they have broken natural laws. We are supposed to breathe
clean air, oxygen. Some people have broken natural laws and
for a lifetime have breathed in the narcotic of nicotine. God
intended our lungs to inhale oxygen. Consequently, in breaking these natural laws of God, many are inflicted with disease
today. Others are sick with cirrhosis of the liver. For many it is
a direct result of breaking natural laws as for years they have
been filling their bodies with alcoholic beverages.

Others are sick because of *demonic attack*. Jesus related the
story in Matthew 17:14-18, "And when they came to the
multitude, a man came up to Him, falling on his knees before
Him, and saying, 'Lord, have mercy on my son, for he is a
lunatic, and is very ill; for he often falls into the fire, and often
into the water. And I brought him to your disciples, and they
could not cure him.' And Jesus answered and said, 'O
unbelieving and perverted generation, how long shall I be
with you? How long shall I put up with you? Bring him here
to Me.' And Jesus rebuked him, and the demon came out of
him, and the boy was cured at once" (NASB).

Others are sick because they have *sin* in their lives. The
Bible records in 1 Corinthians 11:30 "For this reason many

among you are weak and sick, and a number sleep" (NASB). Some are sick because they have sinned. I suppose in our day the number-one example of this type of sickness could be herpes. This venereal disease, which has no known cure, is reported by *Time* magazine to have already infected twenty million Americans, and is growing at a rapid rate. It is the expensive toll taken by those who live in adultery and fornication against the will of God. Obviously, most people would not have contracted this sickness had it not been for illicit affairs. The same is true with the frightful disease, AIDS.

Others are sick because of *physical deterioration.* They simply have grown old, and it is a means of transporting them from earth into heaven.

Jesus also declared that some are sick in order to give *glory to God.* When he heard that Lazarus was sick, he said, "This sickness is not unto death, but for the glory of God" (John 11:4).

Finally, some are sick in order to *bring them to God.* I remember in 1975, while pastoring in Oklahoma, going to the hospital to visit a young, successful businessman in our city. He had no time for God and was caught up in things of the world. His world had come tumbling in as he lay at the point of death with diabetes. Steve Dighton turned his life over to the Lord Jesus Christ and today he is a preacher of the gospel. His sickness was used by God to bring him to Jesus.

Is there any sick among you? Some are sick, not in body, but in spirit. They are spiritually dead without Christ. Others are sick in the realm of the soul, their emotions. There are so many who have deep hurts in their hearts and need the healing touch of the Lord Jesus. And yes, there are others who are sick in body who also need the healing hand of God. The probe! "Is there any sick among you?" One cannot be healed spiritually, emotionally, or physically, until he comes to admit his need. What should one do? Note also:

The Proposal

Let him call for the elders of the church (John 5:14).

Did you notice the proposal? The human initiative comes from the one who is sick. It is the sick person who takes the initiative and the responsibility rests upon him. "Let him call for the elders of the church."

In the New Testament, elders were men called and equipped by the Holy Spirit to serve churches in various capacities. Acts 20:28 says that they were "overseers, to feed the church of God." They were indeed the spiritual leaders of the church.

Now, it is important to note that the Bible is not speaking here about divine-healing ministries or divine-healing crusades. Here is a local church ministry: "Let him call for the elders of the church." There is no suggestion here by James that anyone in the congregation had a "gift of healing." Consequently, these verses have no direct relationship to today's divine healing ministries. This is a local church ministry that unfortunately has been almost totally neglected by the church of the Lord Jesus Christ.

The probe—"Is any sick among you?" The proposal—"Let him call for the elders of the church."

The Procedure

Let them pray over him, anointing him with oil in the name of the Lord (Jas. 5:14).

The procedure is twofold. We are to pray and anoint with oil. James tells us to "let them pray over him." This is a good reminder to all of us who serve in leadership in the church or who hold positions of responsibility. Our duties are not primarily institutional but personal! Our first concern should always be people, not things.

We are to "pray over him." Jesus said, "My house shall be called the house of prayer" (Matt. 21:13). Before the church is to be the house of Bible teaching, evangelism, social action, or any other matter, it is to be called the house of prayer. The only thing the disciples asked the Lord to teach them is recorded in Luke 11:1 when they requested, "Lord, teach us to pray." They lived with him over three years. They had watched his every move. They heard him preach the world's greatest sermons. They had watched him practice everything he preached. They had seen him lead people to himself as no one else before or since had ever done. And after watching his life, they didn't ask him to teach them to evangelize or to teach them to preach or to teach them to minister. They asked, "Lord, teach us to pray." They had discovered that the secret of the life of our Lord Jesus was the time he spent alone with the Father. They evidently knew: if they could ever capture that spirit of prayer they would learn to evangelize, they would learn to preach, they would then learn to minister. The procedure in praying for the sick is that we are to do exactly that, "Pray over him."

The second part of this procedure says that we are to anoint him with oil in the name of the Lord. The general cop-out for this directive is that this was for medicinal purposes. It is true that oil was used in the first-century world for medicinal purposes, but it is not so here. What is it that saves the sick? It is Jesus through the prayer of faith. Mark 6:13 records that Jesus' disciples "cast out many devils, and anointed with oil many that were sick, and healed them." Oil was not used medicinally but symbolically. The cure did not result from the properties of the oil but from the power of the Lord.

In the New Testament, in praying for the sick, oil was used as a visual aid to help focus the faith of the sufferer. You may say, "But Jesus would not need a visual aid." Well, the Lord Jesus often used visual aids in his ministry of healing. It is certainly nothing new in the ministry of our Lord. Remember the account of Mark 7:31-37? When Jesus healed the blind man, he formed the spittle and placed it on the blind man's eyes. Now, the saliva from his mouth did not heal the blind man. The power of the Lord did. The spittle was simply there to focus the faith of the one in need. Also, recorded in John 9:1-41, Jesus used the visual aid of clay in the healing of another man as he placed clay upon his eyes.

In the life of the Lord Jesus there was no set procedure he used in touching the lives of others. Sometimes he used visual aids; other times he did not. It is important to see that the cure does not come from the properties of the oil, but from the power of the Lord. It has been well pointed out by many that we must take great care in avoiding the magical in search of the miraculous.

The procedure plainly laid out for us in James 5:14 is:—one, pray over him, two, anoint with oil. The procedure could not be more clearly set forth. Now, let's note:

The Prayer

In the name of the Lord: and the prayer of faith shall save the sick (Jas. 5:15).

We are not talking here about just any kind of prayer. We are considering the prayer that specifically is prayer "in the name of the Lord" and is referred to as "the prayer of faith." "In the name of the Lord" is much more than a mechanical repetition. When we offer our petition "in the name of the Lord," then God answers us, not in our own merit but in behalf of the Lord Jesus Christ himself. This is exactly how Peter ministered in Acts 3. He and John were going to the Temple to pray, and as they passed through the Beautiful Gate of the Temple they saw a lame man begging. They replied, "Silver and gold have I none, but such as I have, give I thee. In the name of Jesus Christ of Nazareth rise up and walk" (v. 6). Immediately afterwards Peter began to be rebuked by the religious people of his day. He answered in Acts 3:16 by saying, "His name through faith in his name hath made this man strong." Peter refused all personal praise and pointed it all to Jesus. There is power in the name of the Lord Jesus Christ.

Consider these words from Scripture regarding the power in the name of the Lord. Matthew 18:19-20 says, "Again I say unto you, That if two of you shall agree on earth as touching any thing that they shall ask, it shall be done for them of my Father which is in heaven. For where two or three are gathered together in my name, there am I in the midst of them." John 14:13 says, "And whatsoever ye shall ask in my name, that will I do, that the Father may be glorified in the Son." John 14:14 says, "If ye shall ask any thing in my name, I will do it." John 15:16 says, "Ye have not chosen me, but I have chosen you, and ordained you, that ye should go and bring forth fruit, and that your fruit should remain; that whatsoever ye shall ask of the Father in my name, he may give it you." John 16:23 says, "And in that day ye shall ask me nothing. Verily, verily, I say unto you, Whatsoever ye shall ask the Father in my name, he will give it you."

The truth is, this procedure in praying for the sick is only effective when carried out "in the name of the Lord." In other words, in accordance with his will and his authority.

The second important facet of prayer is to know that it is "the prayer of faith." It is not just any prayer. Many pray for the sick and, as they walk away from the place of prayer, say in their heart, *I wonder if God is really going to do it*. Well, he most likely isn't because they have not prayed the prayer of faith. "But let him ask in faith, nothing wavering. For he that wavereth is like a wave of the sea driven with the wind and tossed" (Jas. 1:6). There are even stronger words to be found in Romans 14:23 which says that "whatsoever is not of faith is sin." Jesus put it well in Mark 11:24 when he said "What things soever ye desire, when ye pray, believe that ye receive them, and ye shall have them."

How do we pray the prayer of faith? We have no faith with which to pray if it is not found in the Word of God. The Bible says, "Faith cometh by hearing, and hearing by the word of God" (Rom. 10:17). (*Rhema* is used here and not *logos*. It is the personalized word of God to you). There is no possible way we can pray the prayer of faith unless we have been alone with God and received a word from him upon which to stand. This is where we obtain our faith, from God's Word. Prayer without the Bible and in particular, a *rhema*, has no direction.

The same principle is revealed to us in 1 John 5: "And this is the confidence that we have in him, that, if we ask any thing according to his will, he heareth us: And if we know that he hears us, whatsoever we ask, we know that we have the petitions that we desired of him" (vv. 14-15). Prayer must be according to God's will. I do not give my children everything they ask, because I know basically what is best for them. To be quite honest, I am extremely glad God has not given me everything I have asked of him. There have been many times in my life when my own personal prejudices and desires have taken precedence over his will for me. I have asked him a thousand times to give me something he had no intention of giving me because he had something far better instead. It sounds exciting and attractive to tell people, "You can have anything you ask." The truth is, that is not biblical. The prayer of faith is grounded in the word that God gives to you, or it is not the prayer of faith.

Now, if you pray "in the name of the Lord" and you pray the "prayer of faith," you will pray God's will! How? Because "faith cometh by hearing, and hearing by the word of God" (Rom. 10:17). You cannot have faith without getting a word from God. And if you get the word from God it is obviously his will.

Some may say that if you have enough faith you can be healed. And if you are not healed, it is because you do not have enough faith. This is simply not true. Jesus taught it was not the amount of faith we have. After all, he stressed that if we had faith "as a grain of mustard seed" (Matt. 17:20; Luke 7:6), we could move mountains. The prayer then is offered in the name of the Lord and it is to be the prayer of faith.

The ultimate purpose of everything is to give the glory to God. All sorts of healings can give God glory. Healing by natural processes gives glory to God. Healing by medicine gives glory to God. Healing in the supernatural realm gives glory to God. Even some deaths can give glory to God for the psalmist wrote, "Precious in the sight of the Lord is the death of his saints" (Ps. 116:15).

The Provision

The prayer of faith shall save the sick, and the Lord shall raise him up; and if he have committed sins, they shall be forgiven him (Jas. 5:15).

Most of us would not have a problem with this verse had James said, "The prayer of faith *may* save the sick, and the Lord *may* raise him up." But the Bible reads, "The prayer of faith shall save the sick, and the Lord shall raise him up." Why do we find it so hard to believe that Jesus is the same today as he was yesterday? The truth is that far more people should be healed than are being healed because of our lack of faith.

This brings us to a pivotal question. Is everyone supposed to be healed? What is the meaning of Matthew 8:17: "Himself took our infirmities, and bare our sicknesses"? Some argue that because of the cross everyone should be healed, and if they are not it is either because of sin or a lack of faith. Let me ask you, do you have complete possession *here and now* of all the benefits of the Lord's death? Do you? Are you free from temptation? Now it is true that because of his death you will be ultimately free, but you still must face it now. Are you free from death, sorrow, pain? Now, it is true, because of his death, that ultimately you will be, but you still must face it now—right? For the now we are living with natural, physical limitations. Although death for the Christian has indeed lost its sting, as Paul tells us in 1 Corinthians 15, it is still something we must experience on this earth if Jesus does not return soon. The same is true with bodily sickness. But our biggest problem is a prejudicial aversion to praying the prayer of faith over the sick. If more of God's people would begin calling on the church to pray for their sicknesses, and if more churches would accept their local church ministry with fervor and expectation, God would unleash untold blessings upon the church and many would be healed to God's glory.

At this point I want to dispel a fallacy that if someone is sick it is because of sin in his or her life. This may or may not be the case, but it certainly is not the case in every situation as some people teach. Recall the account in John 9 of the blind man? Jesus declared such was not so. The people asked Jesus, "Who did sin, this man, or his parents, that he was born blind?" (v. 2). Jesus emphatically replied, "Neither hath this man sinned, nor his parents" (v. 3).

This causes us to face another question. Is it God's will that everyone be healed? The truth is that it is God's will that far more people be healed than are being healed but, in my opinion, it is not accurate to claim that it is God's will that everyone be healed. Why did Paul in 2 Timothy 4:20 say that he "Left Trophimus at Miletum sick," instead of healing him? Why did Paul in Philippians 2:27 allow Epaphroditus to become "sick nigh death" instead of pointing out the one sure remedy of healing? Why did Paul in 2 Corinthians 12:9 ask the Lord three times to remove the thorn in his flesh only to hear the Lord say, "My grace is sufficient for thee" instead of being healed? Why did Paul in 1 Timothy 5:23 write to Timothy and say, "Use a little wine for thy stomach's sake"? While God *can* preserve and restore any of his people from sickness, it is plainly *not always* his will to do so. However, if we want to look at extremes I am certainly convinced that most of us have avoided even asking for the supernatural.

What does all this mean? The probe? The proposal? The

procedure? The prayer? The provision? It means that God is
sovereign. He always does what he pleases and is always
pleased with what he does. He is the healer! Sometimes he
heals instantly. All healing is divine. A physician does not
heal, nor does medicine heal, nor does a proper diet heal, nor
does the right environment heal. It is all from God. He is the
healer. Fresh air is his gift to us. Vitamins and minerals are
the gifts of God. Medicine is the gift of God. The surgeon's
skill is the gift of God. Some contend that going to the doctor
shows a lack of faith. This is not only untrue—it is foolish.
Paul wrote in Colossians 4:14 about "Luke, the beloved
physician." Here is a clear inference that as a man of God,
Luke was still recognized as an able physician. He was neither
looked down upon nor ridiculed for his profession.

Our part then is to pray. We are to pray and trust God. And
we are to pray in the name of the Lord and pray the prayer of
faith. If you were sick—I mean really sick—and called on me
to come and pray at your sickbed, would you want me to pray,
"Lord, bless this dear brother and help him to live with these
circumstances." Or, if you were really sick and in pain, would
you want me to pray, "Lord, in the name of Jesus, we believe
that you are the healer. Lord, put your warm hand of healing
upon this body right now and raise him up in Jesus' name."
You see, "We are coming to a king, large petitions with us
bring. For his grace and power are such that one could never
ask too much."

It is time for the church of the Lord Jesus Christ to begin
doing what the Scripture teaches. One fact is for certain—it is
always God's will for his people to pray. There are people who
direly need physical healing. There are others who are in
need of emotional healing. There is still a great host of others
who are in need of spiritual healing. "Is any sick among you?
Let him call for the elders of the church and let them pray
over him, anointing him with oil in the name of the Lord, and
the prayer of faith will save the sick."

Perhaps you need to enter the place of prayer in behalf of someone who is spiritually sick. That is, a person who is lost without Christ, who unless he turns to Christ will never experience the free pardon of sin and the eternal happiness that awaits them. Perhaps you need to pray in behalf of someone who is emotionally sick, whose feelings are hurt by open wounds and emotional scars. Jesus can heal the emotionally sick. Maybe you should come to the place of prayer in behalf of someone who is physically sick. Luke gave the account of four men who brought their friend to Jesus on a pallet, cut a hole in the roof, and lowered him into Jesus' presence. The Bible says when Jesus saw "their faith" he said to the man, "Rise up and walk" (Luke 5:20,23).

The probe? Is there any sick among you? The proposal? Let him call for the elders of the church. The procedure? The spiritual leaders of the church then are to pray over him, anointing him with oil. The prayer? The prayer is to be offered in the name of the Lord Jesus and it is to be the prayer of faith. The provision? The Lord will save the sick and raise him up. Note carefully: the Lord is the healer. "Said I not unto thee, that, if thou wouldest believe, thou shouldest see the glory of God?" (John 11:40).

7.
Robbery Without a Weapon

Even from the days of your fathers ye are gone away from mine ordinances, and have not kept them. Return unto me, and I will return unto you, saith the Lord of hosts. But ye said, Wherein shall we return? Will a man rob God? Yet ye have robbed me. But ye say, Wherein have we robbed thee? In tithes and offerings. Ye are cursed with a curse: for ye have robbed me, even this whole nation. Bring ye all the tithes into the store-house that there may be meat in mine house, and prove me now herewith, saith the Lord of hosts, if I will not open you the windows of heaven, and pour you out a blessing, that there shall not be room enough to receive it. And I will rebuke the devourer for your sakes, and he shall not destroy the fruits of your ground; neither shall your vine cast her fruit before the time in the field, saith the Lord of hosts. And all nations shall call you blessed: for ye shall be a delightsome land, saith the Lord of hosts (Mal. 3:7-12).

Why is it that when E. F. Hutton talks about money "everybody listens," but when the preacher mentions it everybody tunes him out? As farfetched as it may seem, our finances generally mark the position of our spiritual pilgrimage. We are no farther along in our walk with God than the point to which we have learned to trust him with the tithe. Pastor Richard Jackson has well put it, "More could be learned about a person's commitment by looking at their checkbook than their prayer book." This one area could be the reason for many unresolved conflicts and unmet needs.

The tithe is the place where many Christians go astray; some because they have never been taught the spiritual truths concerning stewardship; others because they have not studied the Word of God to find these truths for themselves. But mostly, I suppose, because of willful rebellion against the Word of God. Many Christians profess to love the Bible and take it as their rule of faith and practice, and yet deliberately ignore the plain teaching of the Word of God regarding the tithe.

This chapter is not designed to "get more money for the church or for God's work." It is designed to lead the reader into spiritual growth and blessing by his being obedient to the Word of God. One of the common complaints about many preachers is that "they are always preaching about money." It is usually a telltale sign that those making these statements are generally the ones who are disobedient to God's Word regarding the tithe. This is certainly one area where a lot of modern-day "angels" fear to tread.

There is plenty of misunderstanding concerning the tithe (one tenth of our income belonging to God). In fact, one of the gross injustices many of us preachers have done to the church is to insist that God demands one tenth of our income and one seventh of our week. This implies that the other nine tenths of our income and the other six days of the week are ours to do with as we please. The truth of the matter is that everything we have belongs to God. Not just the tenth— everything! We are nothing more than stewards, passing through this world. For most of us, fifty years from now everything we own will be in someone else's name. Fifty years ago what we own today belonged to someone else, our land, our home, our assets. When we came into this world, we were naked and without a dime, and the unvarnished truth which follows is that we will leave this world the same way. We don't own a thing. We are merely stewards of God's resources. Consequently, the tithe is a splendid place to start in our stewardship with God, but it is a terrible stopping place.

As the Word of God unfolds before us, we will see that its whole emphasis is not on our giving as much as it is on God's opening the windows of heaven to pour us out a blessing that there will not be room enough to receive it. God wants to bless us far more than we want a blessing. The tithe is a starting place in getting God into action in the affairs of man. Let's venture into the realm of this exciting journey with God that promises to "open for you the windows of heaven and pour out for you a blessing until it overflows" (v. 10, NASB).

We note first:

God's Apparent Problem With Us!

Even from the days of your fathers we are gone away from mine ordinances, and have not kept them. Return unto me, and I will return unto you, saith the Lord of hosts. But ye said, Wherein shall we return? Will a man rob God? Yet ye have robbed me. But ye say, Wherein have we robbed thee? In tithes and offerings. Ye are cursed with a curse; for ye have robbed me, even this whole nation. (Mal. 3:7-9).

We have before us God's problem with us. We see initially that this problem is *personal*. "Ye have robbed me!" (Note the personal pronouns.) Have you ever been the victim of robbery? I talked recently with one of the women in our church whose home had been robbed; her dresser drawers ransacked, money stolen, along with valuable papers, and many sentimental items of great value, including the wedding ring of her deceased husband. Her anguish was intensified by the fact that someone uninvited had invaded the privacy of her domain and took items of value which belonged to her. Robbery is a most personal matter, and only one who has been a victim of such an experience can understand the real anguish of heart. God's apparent problem with us is personal. He said, "Ye have robbed me!" This is a strong accusation and not a mere insinuation. He calls to us in Malachi 3:7, saying, "Return unto me, and I will return unto you." The point of return is always the point of departure. If we return, we must return to the place of our departure. And God says that the place of departure for many of us is the matter of the tithe.

Here is God's apparent problem with us. It is robbery without a weapon. "*You* have robbed *me!*" But the truth is: when we rob God there are some other items we rob in the process. When we do not faithfully bring the tithe to God, we rob the church of its ministry. We also rob the world of great missionary enterprises of the gospel. But even more personally, we rob ourselves of giant blessing. "It is more blessed to give than to receive" (Acts 20:35).

In the New Testament we find these words escaping the lips of our Lord, "Render therefore unto Caesar the things which are Caesar's; and unto God the things that are God's" (Matt. 22:21). Isn't it amazing that some church members would never entertain the thought of not paying their taxes (that is rendering unto Caesar the things that are Caesar's). Many of us would never think of not paying taxes on our houses, sales taxes, or internal revenue taxes. And yet, many of us never render unto God the things that are God's! This is God's apparent problem with us. It is a personal problem. We have robbed him.

As the text unfolds we see that the problem is not only personal, but it is also *pointed*. God says "Ye have robbed me." We answer back, "How have we robbed thee?" And his answer comes pointedly, "In tithes and offerings." Tithing is God's appointed program for us. It always has been and always will be. There are some who alibi that the tithe is merely an Old Testament law and is not applicable for this dispensation of grace. The fact is: the tithe existed among the people of God long before the law was given. In Genesis 14:20 we view Abraham giving tithes to Melchizedek. In Genesis 28:19-22 we see Jacob vowing to give a tenth unto the Lord. When the law was given, the tithe was definitely incorporated in it. "And all the tithe of the land, whether of the seed of the land, or of the fruit of the tree, is the Lord's: it is holy unto the Lord" (Lev. 27:30).

In the New Testament Jesus approved and no doubt practiced the tithe. The Pharisees were out to catch him at any point they could. Certainly had Jesus been failing on the matter of the tithe, he would have had stern fingers of accusation pointed in his direction. Note what he says in his rebuke of the Pharisees in Matthew 23:23, "Woe unto you, scribes and Pharisees, hypocrites! for ye pay tithe of mint and anise and cummin, and have omitted the weightier matters of the law, judgment, mercy, and faith: these ought ye to have done, and not to leave the other undone." This verse is often misunderstood and misinterpreted. Here Jesus is rebuking the Pharisees for their hypocrisy not for their tithing. In fact he says, "These things ought ye to have done." The word *ought* is an imperative and is translated in other versions as *must*. Jesus saw the tithe as a requirement from God. It is unthinkable, in light of the cross on which our Savior died, that any of us under grace would give less than the Jews gave under law!

I am amazed at many churches' mentality concerning the tithe. Some churches even hand out pledge cards during stewardship campaigns asking the people to sign their names on a card promising to give an amount that "moves toward the tithe" or to pledge a certain amount that is not a tithe. This is astounding that we would ask people to promise to rob God!

It is helpful to know that the tithe is holy unto the Lord. "And all the tithe of the land, whether of the seed of the land, or of the fruit of the tree, is the Lord's: it is holy unto the Lord" (Lev. 27:30). The Bible says that the tithe is *holy* unto the Lord. That is to say, God reserves for himself, as his own, one tenth of what he gives to us. It is holy unto him. Now there are not many persons or things called holy in the Word of God. When something is set aside as holy it is a dangerous thing to keep that from the Lord. You may say, "But I can't afford to tithe." The reason you think you can't is doubtlessly because you have robbed God of something that is holy to him.

Note also that Leviticus 27:30 says, "The tithe . . . *is* the Lord's!" This ought to open our eyes to a misconception that has blinded many from the truth of Scripture. The fact is: one tenth of our income is not our own personal property at all. It does not belong to us. We have no say-so about it whatsoever. The tithe is the Lord's! I didn't say it, God said it! Regardless of what we have done with it, it is the Lord's. God's tithe may be on your back in the form of new clothes. It may be at your home in the form of a new video game for your television set. You may be watching the Lord's tithe each evening on a new color television set in your den. You may be driving the Lord's tithe down the street in the form of a new car. You may be investing the Lord's tithe in a bank or other investment institutions. You may be stealing it, robbing it, driving it, wearing it, investing it, but it is still not yours—the tithe is the Lord's!

Yes, we need to change our mentality so we can give the tithe. No, the tithe is the Lord's. God says that to withhold the tithe is the same as robbing his own treasury. The tithe belongs to God and in reality we do not give anything to him until we give over the tithe.

It is indeed a penetrating question, "Will a man rob God?" Friend, I would rather rob the First National Bank than to rob God. It doesn't matter who we are or what we have, we need to tithe. The worse our financial condition the more we need to tithe. The tithe is holy. It is the Lord's. There is a blessing when we give it and a curse when we steal it, according to the Bible. The Bible warns us plainly: do not touch the tithe! We tithe because we love the Lord Jesus Christ. A Christian should tithe for the same reason he keeps all the other Commandments. If we render unto Caesar the things that are Caesar's, let us also render unto God the things that are God's. Here is God's apparent problem with us. It is personal and it is pointed.

Let us note also:

God's Appointed Program for Us!

Bring ye all the tithes into the storehouse, that there may be meat in mine house, and prove me now herewith, saith the Lord of hosts, if I will not open you the windows of heaven, and pour you out a blessing, that there shall not be room enough to receive it (Mal. 3:10).

If we are indeed guilty of robbing God of the tithe, then there certainly must be a program of rehabilitation to align us into right relationship with him. God lays down this appointed program for us in the text. Notice first, *the plan*.

"*Bring* ye all the tithes into the storehouse." Every word of Scripture is important. God told us to bring the tithes, not send them. The Wise Men did not send their gifts of gold, frankincense, and myrrh to the Christ child—they brought them! The woman with the alabaster box did not send the box for Jesus' anointing—she brought it! God says that we are to bring the tithe. In the act of bringing there is personal worship. This is God's plan—"bring."

Second note *the person*. "Bring *ye* all the tithes into the storehouse." *You* bring! You bring the tithe because you are commanded to bring it and love obeys. John Bisagno, in his book, *The Word of the Lord*, observed "All through the Scripture love is equated with action." Jesus asked, "Lovest thou me? . . . Feed my sheep." At another time he asked, "Lovest thou me? . . . keep my commandments." He said, "He that heareth my words and doeth them, he it is who loveth me." Love is something we do. Love doesn't just sing, "Oh, how I love Jesus"—love tithes! You can tithe without loving, but you cannot love without tithing!

I am always a little intrigued by bumper-sticker evangelism. We have all seen the bumper stickers that declare, "Honk if you love Jesus." However, the latest ones contain far more truth. They say, "Tithe if you love Jesus—anybody can honk!"

Third, note *the proportion* in God's appointed program for us. "Bring ye all the *tithes* into the storehouse." First Corinthians 16:1-2 says: "Now concerning the collection for the saints, as I have given order to the churches of Galatia, even so do ye. Upon the first day of the week let every one of you lay by him in store, as God hath prospered him." Look at those words, "as God hath prospered him." This signifies a definite proportion of income—"as God hath prospered him." It does not say let everyone lay by in store "as he feels led!" Nor does it say let everyone lay by in store "as he feels moved by the Holy Spirit." Friend, the Holy Spirit will never lead us to do anything contrary to the Word of God. And the Word of

God teaches us that the tenth is the Lord's. The Bible plainly says let everyone lay by him in store "as God hath prospered him." That is, in a proportionate way, according to a percentage basis. This makes giving equal. The millionaires and less wealthy persons are equal in their giving in relationship "as God hath prospered." Thus we see that the proportion of our giving is the tithe.

The text then reveals to us *the place* of our tithes. "Bring ye all the tithes into the *storehouse*." Where is the storehouse? Again, 1 Corinthians 16:1-2 says we are to "lay . . . in *store*." This clearly points us back to Malachi 3:10 which says for us to "Bring all the tithes into the storehouse." Also see when we are to do this. "Upon the first day of the week." Now, what happens on the first day of the week? The local New Testament church is at worship, and the truth of the Scriptures is that the local church is the storehouse! In the New Testament over 90 percent of the time when the word *church* is mentioned it refers to that local, first-day worshiping, body of baptized believers. It is not our privilege to scatter our tithe around to all sorts of parachurch organizations, evangelism organizations, youth groups, and the like. They are to receive offerings, not tithes! The tithe is to be brought to the storehouse on the first day of the week. That is, the local New Testament church. And by the way, don't sell the church short. It will still be here when all the other organizations and groups are gone. Any organization that does not originate in, cooperate with, and build up the local New Testament church will come to nought. The place of the tithe is the storehouse, the local church.

The text also reveals to us *the purpose*. "Bring ye all the tithes into the storehouse that there may be meat in mine house." The purpose of bringing the tithe is to further the work of Christ through the church in bringing salvation to men and women. This is our good and godly purpose given to us by the Lord Jesus Christ in the Great Commission.

Finally, note *the proposition*. "Bring ye all the tithes into the storehouse that there may be meat in mine house, and prove me." This is unbelievable! God is saying to you, "Put me [Almighty God] on trial. Prove me, try me, with the tithe!" Here is the only directive in Scripture that can be put on a trial basis. "Try me, prove me," God challenges. We are admonished to return to him the one tenth that is rightfully his and see whether or not he will let us be the losers. Here is an amazing condescension—that God allows himself to be put on trial by us in such a manner. If there is any doubt as to God's existence here is how to prove him. What a proposition—"Prove me, prove me, put me to the test!"

God's appointed program for us is definitely the tithe. The tithe is a grand place to start but a miserable place to stop in our stewardship. In fact, in the purest biblical sense, a tither is simply a reformed thief.

What happens when we become aware of God's apparent problem with us, and meet the conditions of God's appointed program for us? Consider finally:

God's Abundant Promise to Us!

Bring ye all the tithes into the storehouse, that there may be meat in mine house, and prove me now herewith, saith the Lord of hosts, if I will not open you the windows of heaven, and pour you out a blessing, that there shall not be room enough to receive it. And I will rebuke the devourer for your sakes, and he shall not destroy the fruits of your ground; neither shall your vine cast her fruit before the time in the field, saith the Lord of hosts. And all nations shall call you blessed: for ye shall be a delightsome land, saith the Lord of hosts (Mal. 3:10-12).

Oh, the promises of God that are ours for the claiming! We see first that there is *the promise of provision*. God says to us that he "will . . . open you the windows of heaven, and pour you out a blessing, that there shall not be room enough to receive it." There has never been a time when we more needed knowledge of how to open the windows of heaven. Remember, these promises are contingent upon our returning to God in the matter of the tithe.

Please understand that this promise of provision involves *quality*. These blessings come right out of heaven. They are supernatural. God says, "I will . . . open you the windows of heaven, and pour you out a blessing." He will "pour out." They will be sudden. Have you ever poured tea from a pitcher? If you are not careful it will pour out in rapid force. God says our promise of provision will be right out of heaven. What does it mean that he will "open you the windows of heaven?"

Let's let Scripture interpret Scripture. Listen to Genesis 7:11-12: "In the six hundredth year of Noah's life, in the second month, the seventeenth day of the month, the same day were all the fountains of the great deep broken up, and the windows of heaven were opened. And the rain was upon the earth forty days and forty nights." Here the identical expression is used. This same expression used with the deluge of the flood is the same employed in Malachi 3 in God's response to our tithe. God has promised to honor us with an abundant outpouring! And we are not talking about spiritual blessings only, but temporal blessings.

The truth of the Scriptures is that we reap what we sow. If we sow oats, we will reap oats. If we sow wheat, we will reap wheat. The laws of the harvest, simply stated, are that we always reap *what* we sow, we always reap *after* we sow, and we always reap *more than* we sow. Surely we do not suppose the Lover of our souls will allow us to be the losers. Certainly not because we are faithful to his Word and obedient to his will. I have never seen or heard of a consistent tither who did not find this to be true. The reason so many are in financial straits is the simple fact that they have robbed God.

The promise of provision not only involves quality but also *quantity*. Notice the quantity of the blessing: "there shall not be room enough to receive it." This means we shall have to give it away. This more-than-enough blessing is for all who meet God's conditions. Isn't this a far cry from the haunting need where so many are crying "not enough!" Man's rebellion leads to this kind of economy, the cry of not enough! But not God's. His abundant promise to us is that he will open the windows of heaven and pour out a blessing for us we will not have room enough to receive. This is the John 6 principle in action. (The boy gave his lunch of a few "fish sandwiches," and thousands of people were fed and basketsful were left over.) John Bunyan reportedly said, "There was a man; some called him mad; the more he gave; the more he had!" This is God's promise of provision in a nutshell, involving quality along with quantity.

But there is also *the promise of protection* involved here. God says, "I will rebuke the devourer for your sakes." Here is quite a promise! When we return to God with the tithe, we step into the supernatural protection of God. I'll confess to you that I do not know all the ramifications of this promise, but that does not mean I do not choose to abide in them. It is a promise that God will supernaturally give protection. If the devourer is a plague on our crops, God says he will devour it. If the devourer is recession, God says "I will rebuke it in your behalf." God gives supernatural protection to the consistent tither. It is his abundant promise to us.

Now, we are commanded to tithe not because God is dependent upon our gifts of money. This would promulgate the wrong concept of our sovereign God. He certainly is not dependent upon you or me. The truth is, God doesn't need our money. He commands us to tithe in order that we might become involved in his program of economy that unlocks the floodgates of blessing upon us. The whole significance of this passage of Scripture is: when the tithe is presented it releases the vast treasures of heaven and moves God into action in our behalf. It always has and it always will!

God's apparent problem with us is plain. It is personal, "Ye have robbed me." It is pointed, "in tithes." But God doesn't leave us in this sad condition, for we see God's appointed program for us. The plan, "bring"; the person, "ye"; the proportion, "all the tithes"; the place, "into the storehouse"; the purpose, "that there may be meat in mine house" and the proposition, "and prove me." Almighty God is saying to us, "put me on trial, prove me with the tithe!" And once we have met this program we see God's abundant promise to us. The promise of provision and the promise of protection. "If you return to me . . . I'll return to you." Here is God's promise to us today.

The tithe is the Lord's. It is holy unto him. And he led the way. The greatest stewardship verse in the Word of God is found in John 3:16, "For God so loved the world, that he gave his only begotten Son, that whosoever believeth in him should not perish, but have everlasting life." In light of this cross upon which our Savior died the question of our text has penetrating proportions. "Will a man rob God?"

We have come once again to the end of a volume. I trust these pages have been an encouragement to you and that, as you rejoice in Christ's victory, you will not be afraid to stand for him—*where angels fear to tread*!